Annotated Teacher's Edition

. . . a resource of student activities to accompany the *Write on Track* handbook

WRITE SOURCE®

GREAT SOURCE EDUCATION GROUP
a Houghton Mifflin Company
Wilmington, Massachusetts

A Few Words About the *Write on Track SkillsBook*

Before you begin . . .

The *SkillsBook* provides you with opportunities to practice editing and proofreading skills presented in the *Write on Track* handbook. The handbook contains guidelines, examples, and models to help you complete your work in the *SkillsBook.*

Each *SkillsBook* activity includes a brief introduction to the topic and examples showing how to complete that activity. You will be directed to the page numbers in the handbook for additional information and examples. The "Proofreading Activities" focus on punctuation, the mechanics of writing, usage, and spelling. The "Sentence Activities" provide practice in sentence combining and in correcting common sentence problems. The "Language Activities" highlight each of the eight parts of speech.

On Track

On Track Most exercises include an On Track activity at the end of the exercise. The purpose of the On Track activity is to provide ideas that will help you apply what you have learned in your own writing.

Authors: Pat Sebranek and Dave Kemper

Printed in the United States of America

International Standard Book Number: 0-669-48224-2 (student edition)

1 2 3 4 5 6 7 8 9 10 -POO- 05 04 03 02 01

International Standard Book Number: 0-669-48225-0 (teacher's edition)

1 2 3 4 5 6 7 8 9 10 -POO- 05 04 03 02 01

Table of Contents

Proofreading Activities

Using Punctuation

Checking Mechanics

Proofreading Activities

Checking Your Spelling

Using the Right Word

Sentence Activities

Sentence Basics

Sentence Problems

Sentence Combining

Language Activities

Nouns

Pronouns

Verbs

Adjectives and Adverbs

Prepositions, Conjunctions, Interjections

Parts of Speech

1

Proofreading Activities

The activities in this section include sentences that need to be checked for punctuation, mechanics, and usage. Each activity includes a handbook link—a page or pages in *Write on Track* to be used as a guide for the activity.

Name ______________________________

Periods 1

Handbook Link

A **period** is just a little dot, but it has a lot of important uses.

- For one thing, a period is used at the end of a sentence that makes a **statement.**

  Frogs begin their lives in the water.
  Later, they live on land.
  Frogs are amphibians.

- A period is also used at the end of a **request.**

  Please look up "amphibian" in the dictionary.
  Find out what the word means.

1 **Put an *S* in front of each statement, and put an *R* in front of each request. End each sentence with a period. The first one has been done for you.**

S 1. Most frogs are expert swimmers.

S 2. Frogs get much of their power from their strong back legs.

R 3. Do the frog kick next time you are in the water.

R 4. Draw your legs up to your sides.

R 5. Then push them straight back.

S 6. You will move forward just as a frog does.

S 7. You might enjoy swimming this way.

S 8. Frogs wouldn't swim in any other way.

2 **The following paragraph has nine sentences in it. Find the nine sentences. Put a capital letter at the beginning of each one and a period at the end of each one. The first sentence has been done for you.**

Some frogs have homes that are high off the ground. These frogs live in trees. Tree frogs like leafy homes. Many tree frogs are green. Not all of them are green. Some are yellow, red, or orange. Others have stripes and spots. Tree frogs live in all parts of the world. You may have some in your neighborhood.

On Track **Write two sentences. In the first one, state something that a frog can do. In the second one, tell a friend to do something that a frog does.**

1. *Statement* Answers will vary.

2. *Request*

Name ______________________________

Handbook Link
294

Periods 2

Put a **period** after an initial in a person's name. Also use a period after an abbreviation and as a decimal point in a number.

Carl B. Picklefoot	M. Jennifer Jump
Mr. Picklefoot	Foster Ave.
$1.25	3.5 pounds

1

Put periods after the initials in Samantha's name. Then write your name in all of these ways.

Samantha R. ______ Answers will vary. ______

Samantha J. Rowe ______________________

S. J. Rowe ______________________

S. J. R. ______________________

2

Put periods after the abbreviations in these sentences.

1. Where does Mr. Brown live?

2. He used to live on W. Water St., but now he has moved.

3. His new home is on E. Carver Ave., next door to Ms. Trout.

4. Ms. Trout is a dentist, so she is also Dr. Trout.

5. One of Mr. Brown's other neighbors is Lt. O'Malley, a police officer.

6. Many of the homes on E. Carver Ave. were built by J. J. Builders.

3

Put periods where they belong in the paragraph below. (There are 11 periods missing.) The first sentence has been done for you.

Mr. Henry J. Picklefoot went to E. Lancaster to visit his cousin, Ms. Mary W. Bristle. Ms. Bristle works at a movie theater in E. Lancaster. The theater is on W. Broad St., just past J. J. Pollacco's Pizza Palace. While Ms. Bristle was working, Mr. Picklefoot went to three movies. Each one cost $ 7.0 0. The next day, Mr. Picklefoot decided to go back home to W. Lancaster. He had seen enough movies.

On Track

Write two names that include abbreviations or initials. Write two numbers with decimal points. (You can find this information in a magazine or newspaper.) Then write two sentences using these names and numbers.

Names

Numbers with Decimal Points

Answers will vary.

Sentences

✔ ____________________

✔ ____________________

Name ______________________________

End Punctuation

- A **question mark** follows a question.
  Do you want broccoli for supper?
- An **exclamation point** follows a word or sentence that shows strong feeling.
  Wow! That's a great idea!
- A **period** follows a statement or a request.
  I'm not sure I heard you. Say that again.

Handbook Link

1

Put a period, a question mark, or an exclamation point at the end of each of these sentences.

1. What's good about broccoli ___?___

2. Broccoli is rich in vitamins ___.___

3. It tastes great ___. (or) !___

4. It has a pretty green color ___.___

5. The home gardener finds it easy to grow ___.___

6. Why doesn't everyone eat broccoli ___?___

7. I like it with cheese sauce ___.___

8. Who likes it raw ___?___

9. I do ___!___ I do ___!___

10. Broccoli is definitely my favorite vegetable ___. (or) !___

2 **Put a question mark, an exclamation point, or a period at the end of each sentence in this paragraph.**

My favorite vegetable is carrots. They're so sweet. Do you know how my little brother eats carrots? He puts them in rolls and eats them like hot dogs. It's gross! What is your favorite vegetable? Do you like carrots, too?

On Track **Write three sentences about one of the vegetables listed below. One sentence should make a statement or request, another sentence should ask a question, and the third one should express strong feeling.**

eggplant cabbage asparagus squash corn

1. *Statement* Answers will vary.

2. *Question*

3. *Exclamation*

Name ______________________________

Handbook Link

Commas in a Series

- Use commas between words in a series.

  Most desks are full of papers, pencils, and books.

- Use commas between phrases in a series.

  My dad uses solar calculators, felt-tip pens, and sticky notes.

1 **In each sentence, put commas between the words and phrases in the series.**

1. My mom's desk is covered with letters, bills, and pictures.
2. Paper clips, safety pins, and thumbtacks are in a jar.
3. She keeps rulers, scissors, and a plant on a shelf.
4. The top drawer holds stickers, rubber bands, two checkbooks, and three notepads.
5. The bottom drawer contains spiral notebooks, file folders, and old letters.
6. She keeps pencils, pens, and markers in a can that I made in school.
7. A dictionary, a world atlas, and two telephone directories are placed on another shelf.

On Track **Make a list of things you have in your desk or locker.**

Answers will vary.

Now write a paragraph about the things in your desk or locker. Begin with this topic sentence: Please don't open this desk! Your sentences should include words or phrases in a series.

Answers will vary.

Name ______________________

Commas in Dates and Addresses

Handbook Link

1 **Write the names, addresses, and birth dates (including the year) for three of your classmates or friends. Be sure to use commas correctly.**

Answers will vary.

Name Twila Daniel

Address 344 31st Street

City, State, ZIP Corvallis, OR 97330

Birth Date February 19, 1993

Name ______________________

Address ______________________

City, State, ZIP ______________________

Birth Date ______________________

Name ______________________

Address ______________________

City, State, ZIP ______________________

Birth Date ______________________

2 **Complete each invitation below. Use the names and addresses from the first page in this activity. (Feel free to decorate the invitations.)**

SURPRISE PARTY

Please come to a surprise party for Answers will vary.

Twila Daniel

Date: February 19, 2001

Time: 5 p.m. to 8 p.m.

Address: 344 31st St.

Corvallis, OR 97330

Neighborhood Picnic

Please join Answers will vary.

for an afternoon of fun.

Address: __________

____

Date: __________

Time: __________

Name ______________________________

Handbook Link

Commas in Compound Sentences

Use a **comma** before the connecting word in a compound sentence. Some common connecting words are *and, but,* and *or.*

I study plants in school**,** <u>and</u> I know a lot about them.

I've read about the Venus flytrap**,** <u>but</u> I've never seen one.

1

Underline the connecting word in each of these compound sentences. Put a comma before each connecting word.

1. Most plants get their food from soil but some plants eat insects.
2. The Venus flytrap grows in swamps and it really is a trap for flies.
3. The flytrap looks harmless but it is a danger zone for bugs.
4. The leaves are like traps and they actually have teeth!
5. An insect lands on a flytrap's leaf and the leaf snaps shut.
6. The insect is trapped and it can't get away.
7. Venus flytraps are grown in plant stores or they grow wild.
8. You can feed your Venus flytrap bugs but you shouldn't feed it meat.
9. Meat has salt in it and Venus flytraps don't like salt.

2 **Combine each pair of simple sentences to make a compound sentence. Put a comma before the connecting word. The first one has been done for you.**

1. Computers are fast.
They are fun to use.

Computers are fast, and they are fun to use.

2. Robin wants to use her new computer.
She does not know how to turn it on.

Robin wants to use her new computer, but she does not know how to turn it on.

3. She needs help.
She needs it fast.

She needs help, and she needs it fast.

4. Robin asks Ms. Kadiddle.
She says she will help.

Robin asks Ms. Kadiddle, and she says she will help.

On Track **Write a compound sentence about using a computer.**

Answers will vary.

Name ______________________

Commas to Set Off a Speaker's Words

Handbook Link

Use a **comma** to set off the exact words of a speaker from the rest of the sentence.

Ms. Ayala asked**,** "Who remembers the story of the wolf and the kid?"

"I think I do**,**" answered Jamal.

1 Put commas where they are needed in these sentences.

1. "It was about a mother goat who went to get food for her kid" Jamal said.
2. "That's the beginning" said Sam. "Then the mother told the kid to lock the door and not let anyone in."
3. "Next a wolf knocks on the door and talks sweet like the mother" Jamal said.
4. Sam continued "The kid peeks through the window and sees the wolf."
5. "And he doesn't let the wolf in" said Jamal.
6. Ms. Ayala said "What lesson can you learn from this story?"
7. "Mothers know best" laughed Sam and Jamal.

On Track **Write one more thing Ms. Ayala could have said about the story. Be sure to use a comma where it is needed.**

Ms. Ayala said "

____."

2 Put commas where they are needed in the following sentences.

1. "Let's think of other fables we've read," said the teacher.
2. Jan replied, "I remember the one about the ant and the grasshopper."
3. "Oh, that's where the ant does all the work and the grasshopper is lazy," said Amy.
4. "Yes," said Jan. "The ant saved food for the winter, while the grasshopper wasted time."
5. "There's a lesson there," said the teacher.
6. Amy said, "I think it means we should do our work on time."
7. "Good thinking," said the teacher.

On Track **Write one more thing the teacher might say. Use a comma and quotation marks in your sentence.**

Answers will vary.

Name ______________________________

Handbook Link

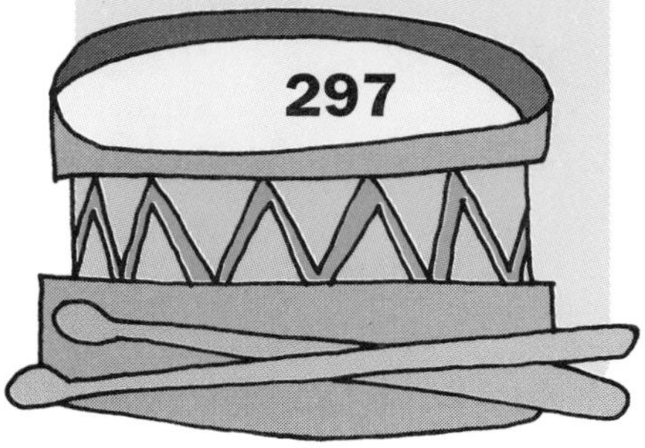

Commas After a Person Spoken To or Introductory Words

- Use a **comma** to set off the name of a person or group being spoken to.

  Class, we're going to have an all-drum band.

- Use a comma to set off an introductory group of words.

  Since drums are noisy, I'll close the door.

1 Add commas where they are needed in these sentences.

1. Josh, you play the conga drum.
2. Yolanda, you take the tom-tom.
3. Tony, here's a tabla drum for you.
4. Elle, you take the big bass drum.
5. Because you play it by hitting it, a triangle is like a drum.
6. Carla, you play the triangle.
7. When you hear all the drums, you'll be amazed at their different sounds.

On Track **Imagine that your class is going to have a band with many different instruments. Write four sentences, each telling a person to play an instrument. (Choose from the instruments below, or come up with your own.) Make sure to use commas correctly. One has been done for you.**

Band instruments

maracas	guitar	flute
tambourine	banjo	piano

1. Todd, you play the tambourine.
2. Answers will vary.
3.
4.
5.

Name ______________________________

Colons

- Use a **colon** after the salutation of a business letter.

  Dear Ms. Cosby: Dear Sir:

- Use a colon between the hours and the minutes in a number that shows time.

  1:15   12:30

Handbook Link

1 Add colons as they are needed in the business letter below.

Dear Mayor Hudson:

I am writing to let you know about our neighborhood's "Cleanup Day." It will take place on Saturday, April 17, from 10:00 a.m. to 4:00 p.m. City trucks will be needed at the following times and places:

11:30 a.m.	City trucks needed to begin picking up bagged trash. It will be placed at street corners throughout the neighborhood.
12:00 noon	Lunch will be donated by El Taco Grande.
4:00 p.m.	City trucks needed to pick up brush cleared at Green Bayou Park. Brush will be piled at the park entrance.

Thank you for your help with this project.

Sincerely,

Matt Stone

Matt Stone

2 **Below are the beginnings of some business letters. Students wrote these letters to confirm plans for field trips. Add colons where they are needed in the letters.**

1. Dear Fire Chief Wilson

Our class is looking forward to visiting the fire station next Monday from 9 3 0 until 1 1 0 0 a.m.

2. Dear Ms. Stephanopoulos

Thank you for inviting us to visit your bakery on Friday between 1 0 3 0 a.m. and 1 2 0 0 noon.

3. Dear Ms. Kennedy

Our class is excited about visiting the TV station from 1 0 0 until 2 0 0 p.m. next Friday.

4. Dear Mr. Alvarez

We are looking forward to our tour of the stadium next Thursday between 1 1 0 0 a.m. and 1 2 3 0 p.m.

On Track **Write the beginning of a letter about a field trip. Write your letter to someone who works at a place you would like to visit. (Make up his or her name.)**

Name ______________________________

Contractions

Handbook Link

An **apostrophe** is used in the spelling of a contraction. The apostrophe takes the place of one or more letters.

Two Words	Contraction
did not	didn't
you are	you're
I am	I'm

apostrophes

1

Write a contraction for each word or word pair in the list. Then rewrite each sentence, replacing the words in bold letters with a contraction.

Two Words	Contraction
is not	isn't
it is	it's
do not	don't
they are	they're
cannot	can't

1. Mary **cannot** sing. Mary can't sing.
2. Jake **is not** singing. Jake isn't singing.
3. **They are** both not singing. They're both not singing.
4. **It is** time for you to sing. It's time for you to sing.
5. But I **do not** want to. But I don't want to.

2

Write contractions for the following word pairs. Then, in each sentence below, write a contraction to replace the words in bold.

Two Words	Contraction	Two Words	Contraction
it is; it has	it's	she will	she'll
I will	I'll	I would	I'd
do not	don't	who is	who's
I am	I'm	was not	wasn't
is not	isn't		

1. **She will** be riding six white horses when she comes. She'll
2. So long, **it has** been good to know you. it's
3. Good night, Irene, **I will** see you in my dreams. I'll
4. If I had a hammer, **I would** hammer in the morning. I'd
5. **Will not** you come home, Bill Bailey? Won't
6. **I am** half crazy, all for the love of you. I'm
7. **Who is** afraid of the big, bad wolf? Who's
8. If they don't win, **it is** a shame. it's
9. It **is not** easy being green. isn't

On Track **The sentences above are lines from songs. Can you sing any of them?**

Name ______________________________

Apostrophes 1

Handbook Link

An **apostrophe** plus an **s** is added to a singular noun to show ownership. (Singular means "one.")

the girl's bike (The bike belongs to the girl.)
the cat's whiskers
(The whiskers belong to the cat.)

1

In each sentence, put an apostrophe in the word that tells who the gerbil belongs to. The first one has been done for you.

1. Chester's gerbil likes leaf lettuce.
2. I think LaJoy's gerbil is the cutest.
3. Where is the teacher's gerbil?
4. Molly's gerbil is under my desk!
5. My neighbor's gerbil stays in a cage.

2

In each sentence, draw a line under the word that tells who the hat belongs to. Draw one of the hats in the box.

1. Who has the baby's hat?
2. Mr. Dandelion's hat is yellow.
3. Look at Roger's hat!
4. Did you see Kathy's red hat?
5. Rocky Stark's hat is black.

3

Combine each set of words into a possessive phrase. Then write an interesting sentence using the phrase. Make sure to use apostrophes correctly. The first one has been done for you.

1. Betty ➤ house Betty's house

   I went to Betty's house to play.

2. my sister ➤ pony my sister's pony

   Answers will vary.

3. our dog ➤ name our dog's name

4. a clown ➤ face a clown's face

5. Mr. Bughopper ➤ car Mr. Bughopper's car

6. a bluebird ➤ house a bluebird's house

7. Shauna ➤ desk Shauna's desk

On Track **Exchange your sentences with a classmate. Check the apostrophes in your partner's work.**

Name ______________________________

Apostrophes 2

- Add **'s** to a singular noun to show ownership. (Singular means "one.")

  the dog's house

- Add an apostrophe after a plural noun ending in **s**. (Plural means "more than one.")

  the dogs' houses

Handbook Link

1 **Add an apostrophe in each phrase below to show ownership. In the blank, tell if the phrase shows singular or plural possession. The first one has been done for you.**

1. Maryanne has one hamster in a cage. You write . . .

the hamster's cage ___singular possession___

2. Claudia has a cage with three hamsters in it. You write . . .

the hamsters' cage ___plural possession___

3. You have a rabbit. The rabbit lives in a hutch. You write . . .

the rabbit's hutch ___singular possession___

4. Your brother gets a rabbit, so you have two rabbits. You write . . .

the rabbits' hutch ___plural possession___

5. The rabbits have babies. You have to get another hutch. You write . . .

the rabbits' hutches ___plural possession___

2 **Put a possessive singular noun in the blank to complete each sentence. The first sentence has been done for you.**

1. Madeline's dog ate my lunch.
2. My Answers will vary. dog likes potato chips.
3. ________ dog barked at me.
4. Where is ________ little dog?
5. I have to walk ________ dog for a week.

On Track **Below is a list of names and the things that belong to each person or group. Combine the two words into a possessive phrase. Then write an interesting sentence using the phrase. The first one has been done for you.**

1. Katie ➤ roller skates Katie's roller skates

   Katie's roller skates have lightning bolts painted on them.

2. Mr. Bluster ➤ cane Mr. Bluster's cane

   Answers will vary.

3. Dolly ➤ wig Dolly's wig

4. the Dolphins ➤ helmets the Dolphins' helmets

5. Diana ➤ gowns Diana's gowns

Name ______________________________

Handbook Link

Quotation Marks 1

One way to show what people say to each other is to use speech balloons.

Another way to show what people say is to use **quotation marks**. The quotation marks set off the exact words of the speaker.

Tom said, **"**Why didn't you call me back last night?**"**
"I'm sorry. We got home very late,**"** Les answered.

1 **Read the words in the speech balloons below. Then, in the sentences that follow, put quotation marks before and after the exact words that Tom and Les said.**

Tom said, "I wanted to ask if you could sleep over Saturday night."

"I hope I can. I'll ask my mom," said Les.

2 **Read the speech balloons that follow. Then, in the space below, write what Tom and Les said, using quotation marks correctly in your sentences.**

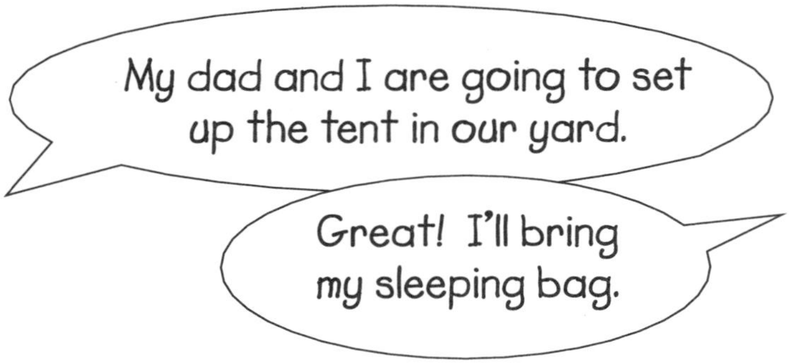

Tom said, "My dad and I are going to set up the tent in our yard."

Les replied, "Great! I'll bring my sleeping bag."

On Track **It's the next day. Tom and Les see each other again. Now you decide what they say. Make sure to use quotation marks correctly.**

Answers will vary.

Name ________________________________

Handbook Link

Quotation Marks 2

When you write **dialogue**, you can name the speaker at the beginning of the sentence, at the end of the sentence, or in the middle of the sentence.

- When the speaker is named at the **beginning** of the sentence, use a comma and quotation marks like this:

  Carla said, “I'm going to camp this summer.”

- When the speaker is named at the **end** of the sentence, use a comma and quotation marks like this:

  “Late at night, we tell ghost stories,” said Camy.

- When the speaker is named in the **middle** of the sentence, use commas and quotation marks like this:

  “Camp starts July 5,” Carla said, “and we stay for two weeks.”

1

Add commas and quotation marks where they are needed in the following sentences. The speaker is named at the beginning of each sentence.

1. Camy said, “I'm going, too.”
2. Josh said, “Won't you miss your parents?”
3. Carla answered, “Yes, but we'll still have fun.”
4. Josh asked, “What are you going to take?”
5. Carla said, “I'm taking a lot of shorts and T-shirts.”

2 **Add commas and quotation marks in the sentences below. The speaker is named at the end of each sentence.**

1. “The ghost stories always scare me a little,” Camy said.
2. “I'd be scared, too,” said Josh.
3. “Aw, they're only fake stories,” said Carla.

3 **Add commas and quotation marks in the following sentences. The speaker is named in the middle of each sentence.**

1. “This summer,” said Carla, “I'm going to learn to dive.”
2. “I can dive,” Camy said, “but not headfirst.”
3. “If it's not headfirst,” said Josh, “it's not a dive.”
4. “If it's belly first,” Josh said, “it's a belly flop!”

On Track **Write two more sentences of dialogue between the campers. Use commas and quotation marks correctly to punctuate your dialogue.**

Answers will vary.

Name ______________________________

Handbook Link
294-302

Punctuation Review

This activity is a review of punctuation marks.

1 **Fill in the blanks in the following sentences. Make sure to use punctuation marks correctly.**

1. Today's date is ______Answers will vary.______ .
2. My school's name is ______________________ .

   My school is in this city and state:

   ____

3. School starts at __________ a.m., and it ends at __________ p.m.
4. Our class is studying ______________________

   ______________ and ______________ .

5. Our teacher's name is ______________________ .

2 **Fill in the blanks in the following sentences. Show each speaker's exact words. Make sure to use commas and quotation marks correctly.**

1. My teacher always says ______Answers will vary.______

   ______________________________________ .

2. I told my friend ______________________

   ______________________________________ .

3 **In each sentence below, add apostrophes and end punctuation. The first sentence has been done for you.**

1. Those rabbits aren't supposed to eat that lettuce, and those raccoons shouldn't be in the birdbath.
2. I'll eat banana pancakes, but I'd rather have blueberry.
3. Haven't you finished your homework, or are you planning to do it in the morning?
4. You won't believe this, but my mom's soup is made out of seaweed.
5. We'll borrow Dad's hammer for five minutes, and then we'll put it back in his toolbox.
6. Don't tell anyone, but I've got candy bars hidden in my pillowcase.
7. I can't find my schoolbag, so may I use your backpack?

On Track **Did you notice that all of the sentences above are compound sentences? Circle the connecting word in each sentence.**

Name ______________________

Handbook Link

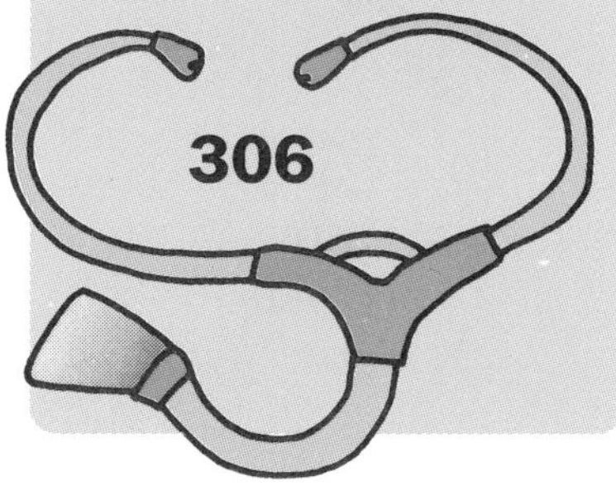

Capitalizing First Words

- Always capitalize the **first word** in a sentence.

  My heart is a muscle.

  Can you hear it beat?

- Capitalize the first word of a direct quotation, too. (A quotation is the words spoken by someone.)

  She said, **"O**nly I can hear it."

1

Capitalize the first word in each sentence below. The first one has been done for you.

1. every animal has a pulse rate.
2. it is measured in heartbeats per minute.
3. big animals have slower pulse rates than little animals.
4. find your pulse.
5. how fast is your heart beating?
6. what do you mean?
7. count the number of times your heart beats in one minute.
8. the average person's heart beats 72 times a minute.
9. runners may have heart rates as low as 35 beats per minute.
10. that's so low!

2

Add capital letters where they are needed in the sentences below. The first one has been done for you.

1. "how fast does your heart beat?" he asked.
2. she answered, "my heartbeat is not as fast as a baby's."
3. he said, "how fast is a baby's heartbeat?"
4. "it's not as fast as a rabbit's," she said.
5. then he asked, "how fast is a rabbit's heartbeat?"
6. she smiled and said, "it's not as fast as a mouse's."

On Track

Write a paragraph explaining why the heart is a sign of love. Make sure to capitalize and punctuate your sentences correctly.

Answers will vary.

Name ______________________________

Capitalizing Proper Nouns

Handbook Link

A **proper noun** names a specific person, place, thing, or idea. A proper noun is always capitalized.

Mary

St. **L**ouis

Strawberry **F**estival

1 Write two proper nouns for each category.

1. city Houston ____ Springfield ____
2. holiday ____ Answers will vary. ____
3. school ____ ____
4. ocean ____ ____
5. person ____ ____
6. park ____ ____

2 Write an interesting sentence using at least two of the proper nouns in your list.

Answers will vary.

____

____

____

3 **Fill in the missing days and months in the two charts below. Remember that days and months are capitalized.**

Days of the Week

1. Monday
2. Tuesday
3. Wednesday
4. Thursday
5. Friday
6. Saturday
7. Sunday

Months of the Year

1. January
2. February
3. March
4. April
5. May
6. June
7. July
8. August
9. September
10. October
11. November
12. December

On Track **Answer the following questions.**

1. What day and month is it today?

   Answers will vary.

2. In what month were you born? ______________________

3. What is your favorite day of the week? ______________________

Name ______________________________

Capitalizing Titles

Capitalize the first word of the **title** of a book or magazine, the last word, and every important word in between.

<u>The Biggest Pancake Ever</u> **(book title)**

Handbook Link

Follow these rules for words in the middle of a title.

- Don't capitalize articles *(a, an, the).*
- Don't capitalize short prepositions *(to, with, by, for).*
- Don't capitalize conjunctions *(and, but).*

<u>Tea with Milk</u> (book)

<u>Amelia and Eleanor Go for a Ride</u> (book)

1 **Write the titles using capital letters in the right places. Because these are names of books and magazines, underline them. The first one has been done for you.**

1. the cat and the fiddle <u>The Cat and the Fiddle</u>

2. penny pollard's letters <u>Penny Pollard's Letters</u>

3. i'm in charge of celebrations
<u>I'm in Charge of Celebrations</u>

4. the dragon's boy <u>The Dragon's Boy</u>

5. song of the trees <u>Song of the Trees</u>

6. ranger rick <u>Ranger Rick</u>

7. highlights for children <u>Highlights for Children</u>

2 Follow each direction by adding titles. Use capital letters correctly. Underline the titles.

✔ Two of my favorite TV shows:

Answers will vary.

✔ Two of my favorite books:

✔ Two of my favorite movies:

✔ When I write my first book, the title will be one of these three:

Name ______________________

Capitalizing Geographic Names

The names of specific rivers, lakes, mountains, cities, states, countries, streets, roads, planets, and highways should be capitalized.

1 **Write three geographic names in each of the columns. Be sure to use capital letters correctly. (You may want to work on this activity with a partner.)**

Rivers	**Lakes**
Answers will vary.	

Cities	**States**

Streets/Avenues	**Planets**

2

Capitalize the geographic names in these sentences. The numbers in parentheses tell you how many capital letters you need to change. The first sentence has been done for you.

1. The town of red lion, pennsylvania, is on the susquehanna river. (5)

2. If you're looking for lake old wives, you'll find it in canada. (4)

3. The hungry horse reservation is in montana. (4)

4. The snake river forms part of the border between idaho and oregon. (4)

5. There's a town in arkansas called bad knob. (3)

6. In ohio you'll find mount healthy. (3)

7. If you ever go to flaydada, texas, you might see the salt fork river. (5)

8. When pumpkin creek joins the tongue river, they flow into the yellowstone river. (6)

9. In new jersey you'll find a city called orange. (3)

10. You'll find lake cadibarrawirracanna in australia. (3)

11. The honey river flows through california. (3)

Name ______________________________

Capitalization Review

This activity is a review of capitalization.

1 **Add capital letters in the following paragraphs. Also answer the question after each paragraph. The first capital letter has been added.**

Handbook Link

Rub It Out

In 1770, an englishman named joseph priestley was traveling in south america. he gathered some of the juice coming from the trees. he found that it would rub out pencil marks. he called it rubber.

What are three things that are made of rubber?

______________ Answers will vary. ______________

Blast It

in sweden, a man named alfred nobel invented a blasting material he called dynamite. miners often use dynamite. money he earned from the invention now goes to people who win the nobel prize.

Why do miners use dynamite?

Miners use dynamite to blast big holes in the earth.

2 **Here are two more paragraphs to capitalize. Also answer the question at the end of each paragraph.**

Weave It

long ago, empress si ling-chi was sipping tea in china. a caterpillar cocoon fell into her cup. she unwound the cocoon and said, "it's made of a long thread. what will happen if I have it woven into cloth?" that's how chinese silk was discovered.

What are two things that are made of silk?

Answers will vary.

Wipe It Off

an american woman, mary anderson, had a good idea in 1903. "aha!" she thought. "if you push a rubber blade across a windshield, you can wipe away rain and snow." what do we call her invention today?

Answer: windshield wiper

Name ______________________________

Handbook Link

Plurals 1

A **plural noun** names more than one thing. Most plurals are formed by adding *s* to the word. But some nouns form their plurals in different ways.

- The plurals of nouns ending in ***sh, ch, x, s,*** or ***z*** are made by adding *es* to the singular.
  brush → brushes fox → foxes glass → glasses
- The plurals of nouns that end in ***y*** (with a consonant just before the ***y***) are formed by changing the ***y*** to ***i*** and adding ***es.***
  baby → babies fly → flies
- The plurals of nouns that end in ***y*** (with a vowel just before the ***y***) are formed by adding only an ***s.***
  day → days monkey → monkeys

1

Write the plural form for each singular noun. The first two have been done for you.

1. boss bosses

2. rabbit rabbits

3. mess messes

4. dish dishes

5. fox foxes

6. ant ants

7. army armies

8. plane planes

9. sky skies

10. donkey donkeys

11. switch switches

12. buzz buzzes

2 **Write the correct plurals in the blanks. The first sentence has been done for you.**

1. Long ago twin ___princesses___ lived in a palace.
(princess)

2. One night two old ___ladies___ came to the gate.
(lady)

3. Each lady carried a pile of ___boxes___ .
(box)

4. "Each box holds three ___wishes___ ," they said.
(wish)

5. The young ___princesses___ opened the gate.
(princess)

On Track **Write a short ending to the story started above.**

Answers will vary.

Name ______________________________

Plurals 2

Handbook Link

A **plural noun** names more than one thing. In this activity, you will practice forming many different plural nouns. (You may use a dictionary with this activity.)

1 Write the plural form for each word listed below.

1. bunch bunches

2. box boxes

3. pitch pitches

4. day days

5. story stories

6. daddy daddies

7. beach beaches

8. glass glasses

9. guess guesses

10. flash flashes

11. jelly jellies

12. key keys

13. candy candies

14. baby babies

2 Write the plural form for each irregular noun below.

1. wolf wolves

2. knife knives

3. mouse mice

4. man men

5. foot feet

6. child children

On Track **Write the plural of each word below. Then write a sentence using the plural form of the word.**

1. *singular:* bush *plural:* bushes

sentence: ______________________

____

2. *singular:* nurse *plural:* nurses

sentence: ______________________

____

3. *singular:* woman *plural:* women

sentence: ______________________

____

4. *singular:* goose *plural:* geese

sentence: ______________________

____

5. *singular:* giant *plural:* giants

sentence: ______________________

____

Name ______________________________

Writing Numbers

Handbook Link

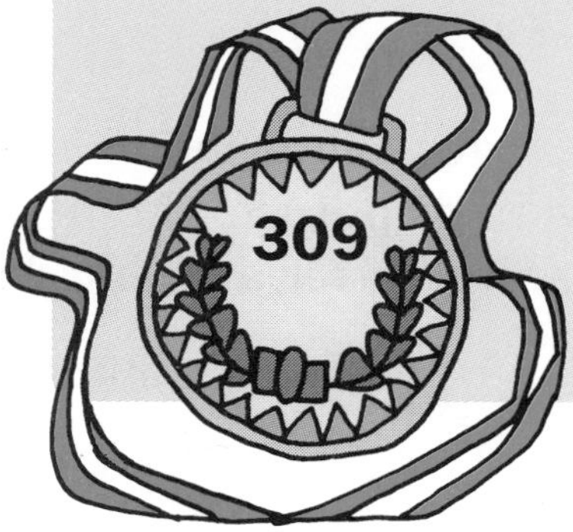

- Numbers from one to nine are usually written as words.

  Runner Marion Jones won five Olympic medals in one year.

- Numbers larger than nine are usually written as numerals.

  The United States has won 46 world titles in figure skating.

TIP: A number at the beginning of a sentence is written as a word.

1

Follow the directions for each sentence. Write your numbers correctly and be sure to use your handbook.

1. Write a sentence telling how old you are.

Answers will vary.

____

2. Write a sentence using a very large number.

____

3. Write a sentence about the number of doors in your classroom.

____

4. Write a sentence naming an amount of money.

____

5. Write a sentence telling how many students are wearing tennis shoes in your class.

____

Name ______________________

Using Abbreviations

Handbook Link

An **abbreviation** is the shortened form of a word or phrase. Many abbreviations begin with a capital letter and end with a period.

Mister = Mr.
Doctor = Dr.
Street = St.

1 **Circle the abbreviations in this address:**

Mr. Michael Carlson, Jr.
222 W. Bridge Ave.
Greenville, NY 01209

TIP: Postal abbreviations for states have two capital letters and no period.

Massachusetts → MA

On Track **Write your name and address here. Use at least two abbreviations.**

Answers will vary.
____
(Name)

____
(Street)

____
(City, State, ZIP)

Name ______________________

Handbook Link

311

State Abbreviations

Each state has a postal abbreviation that has two letters.

Alabama = AL Minnesota = MN
Wyoming = WY Maine = ME

1 **After each set of clues, write the full name of the state. Then write the two-letter abbreviation for the state.**

1. Statue of Liberty, Empire State Building, Niagara Falls	New York	NY
2. Sunshine State, Kennedy Space Center, Everglades	Florida	FL
3. Lone Star State, Alamo, Dallas	Texas	TX
4. San Francisco, redwoods, the gold rush	California	CA
5. St. Louis, Gateway Arch, Lake of the Ozarks	Missouri	MO
6. Phoenix, Grand Canyon, desert	Arizona	AZ
7. Chicago, Abe Lincoln, Lake Michigan	Illinois	IL
8. Atlanta, Peach State, Civil War	Georgia	GA
9. Islands, volcanoes, 50th state	Hawaii	HI
10. Santa Fe, astronomy, Carlsbad Caverns	New Mexico	NM

2 **Make your best guess to answer each question below. Then open your handbook to pages 311 and 379 to check and correct your work.**

Which is the . . .	State Name	Abbreviation
1. largest state?	Alaska	AK
2. smallest state?	Rhode Island	RI
3. state with the highest point?	Alaska	AK
4. state with the rainiest spot?	Hawaii	HI
5. state with the driest desert?	California	CA

On Track **Draw a map of your state. Show the state capital, the city or town you live in, and other interesting places. Label your map with the state's name and its postal abbreviation.**

Name ______________________________

Mechanics Review

Handbook Link
304-311

This activity is a review of capitalization, plurals, numbers, and abbreviations.

1 **Fill in the blanks in the sentences below. Make sure to use capital letters and numbers correctly.**

1. ______Answers will vary.______ is a state I want to visit.

2. ______________________ is my favorite holiday, and ______________________ is my favorite month.

3. The abbreviation of my favorite month is ______________.

4. There are ______________ students in my class.

5. Many third graders are ______________ years old.

6. One of my textbooks is called ______________________, and I am on chapter ______________.

7. My handbook is called ______________________, and one chapter is called "______________________."

8. There are __________ pages in my handbook.

2

Rewrite the addresses below, using as many abbreviations as you can.

Doctor Lee Strong	Dr. Lee Strong
142 South Jefferson Drive	142 S. Jefferson Dr.
River City, Wisconsin 54999	River City, WI 54999
Mister Charles Johnson, Junior	Mr. Charles Johnson, Jr.
3730 Azalea Street West	3730 Azalea St. W.
Wellington, South Carolina 29777	Wellington, SC 29777

3

Write the plural form of each word below. Write it under the rule that explains how to make it plural. The first one has been done for you.

bee	**cow**	**lady**	**crunch**	**splash**
cook	**kitty**	**mess**	**kite**	**fly**

1. Plurals of most nouns are made by adding an *s*.

bees — cooks

cows — kites

2. If a noun ends in *sh, ch, x, s,* or *z,* make the plural by adding *es*.

messes — crunches — splashes

3. If a noun ends in *y* with a consonant just before the *y*, change the *y* to *i* and add *es*.

kitties — ladies — flies

Name ______________________________

Spelling and Alphabetizing

Handbook Link

1

Rewrite the list of birds, putting them in alphabetical (ABC) order. When words begin with the same letter, look at the second and third letters to put them in alphabetical order.

robin	cardinal	eagle
seagull	penguin	hawk
crow	ostrich	loon
albatross	sparrow	swan
bluebird	vulture	duck

1. albatross
2. bluebird
3. cardinal
4. crow
5. duck
6. eagle
7. hawk
8. loon
9. ostrich
10. penguin
11. robin
12. seagull
13. sparrow
14. swan
15. vulture

2

Write the words in alphabetical (ABC) order. When words begin with the same letter, be sure to look at the second and third letters of the words.

1. drive, dressed, dumb

dressed

drive

dumb

2. toward, truth, tonight

tonight

toward

truth

3. might, middle, minute

middle

might

minute

4. bright, bunch, built

bright

built

bunch

5. planet, picture, phone

phone

picture

planet

6. pencil, past, person

past

pencil

person

On Track

On your own paper, write an alphabet poem about something you see or hear around you. See page 178 in your handbook for an alphabet poem about dolphins.

Name ______________________________

Spelling and Silent Letters

Handbook Link
312-315

1 **Choose a word from the list to fill in each blank below. After you write the word, circle the silent consonant or consonants. The first one has been done for you.**

autumn	island	night
calf	knee	rhyme
castle	lamb	write
gnat	listen	

1. The sun shines by day and the moon by night.

2. A baby sheep is called a lamb.

3. When your teacher is talking, it's important to listen.

4. Another name for fall is autumn.

5. A king and a queen are sure to live in a castle.

6. A baby cow is called a calf.

7. Poems and songs often have words that rhyme.

8. A gnat is a tiny bug.

9. It's fun to write letters to friends far away.

10. Your leg bends at the knee.

11. An island is a piece of land surrounded by water.

2

Sort the words below into three groups: one-syllable words, two-syllable words, and three-syllable words.

answer	Friday	knife	right
bought	ghost	middle	science
different	happiness	neighbor	special
dressed	hurry	often	weather
dumb	interest	president	whole
finally	kitchen	probably	would

One-Syllable Words

1. bought
2. dressed
3. dumb
4. ghost
5. knife
6. right
7. whole
8. would

Two-Syllable Words

1. answer
2. Friday
3. hurry
4. kitchen
5. middle
6. neighbor
7. often
8. science
9. special
10. weather

Three-Syllable Words

1. different
2. finally
3. happiness
4. interest
5. president
6. probably

Name ______________________________

Spelling Sorts

Handbook Link 312-315

1 **Sort the words below into two groups. First list all the words that have double consonants. Then list all the words that have silent consonants.**

answer	finally	mirror	tonight
bought	ghost	often	worry
different	guess	really	wrong
dressed	hurry	right	
dumb	knife	science	

Words with Double Consonants

1. different
2. dressed
3. finally
4. guess
5. hurry
6. mirror
7. really
8. worry

Words with Silent Consonants

1. answer
2. bought
3. dumb
4. ghost
5. knife
6. often
7. right
8. science
9. tonight
10. wrong

2 **Using the spelling words on pages 312-315 in your handbook, write the answers to these riddles.**

1. The first meal of the day — breakfast

2. Jack was chased by him. — giant

3. The opposite of awake — asleep

4. Bees make this. — honey

5. A large body of water — ocean

6. 10 X 0 equals . . . — zero

7. Land surrounded by water — island

8. The first month of the year — January

9. The last month of the year — December

10. A small mammal — mouse

11. A color and a fruit — orange

12. The opposite of wrong — right

13. A synonym for "fast" — quick

14. A writer of books — author

15. The plural of "child" — children

On Track **Using the words from the list, write a short story that could make someone laugh.**

Name ______________________________

Using the Right Word 1

Homophones are words that sound the same but have different spellings and meanings. Let's look at three common homophones: *there, their,* and *they're.*

Handbook Link

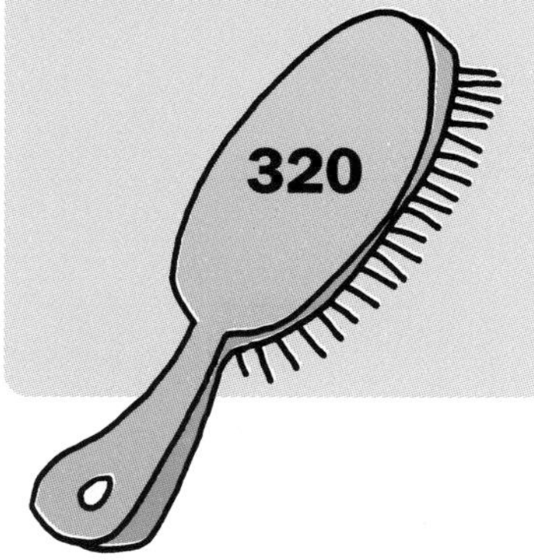

I put my hairbrush **there**.

They use **their** hairbrushes a lot.
(*Their* shows ownership.)

They're brushing their hair.
(*They're* is the contraction for *they are.*)

1

Write the correct word—*there, their,* or *they're*—in each blank.

1. ___There___ are about 100,000 hairs on your head.
2. ___They're___ always growing—about 1/100 of an inch a day.
3. ___They're___ always falling out—from 25-125 hairs a day.
4. ___There___ are many kinds of hair.
5. Many people wish ___their___ hair was curly.
6. Some men lose ___their___ hair and become bald.
7. ___There___ are hairs inside your nose to keep out dust and dirt.
8. The hairs on your head are ___there___ to help block the sun.
9. Many people like to wear ___their___ hair very short.

2 Write two sentences using the word *they're.*

1. Answers will vary.

2.

Write two sentences using the word *there.*

1. Answers will vary.

2.

Write two sentences using the word *their.*

1. Answers will vary.

2.

Name ______________________________

Handbook Link

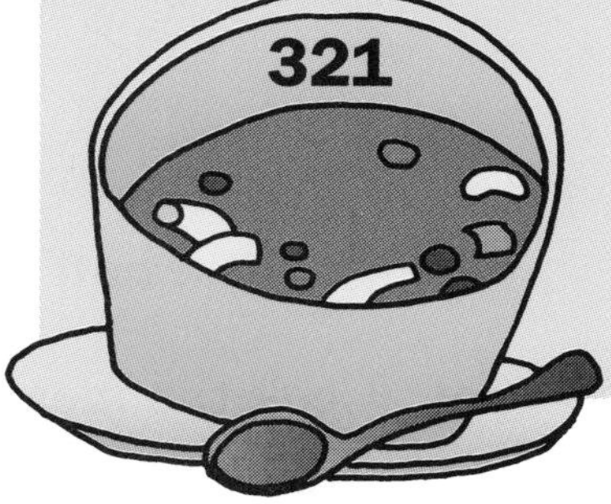

Using the Right Word 2

Homophones are words that sound alike but have different spellings and different meanings. Let's look at three common homophones: *two, to,* and *too.*

For **two** years, Harry went **to** the Chili Contest.

Matilda went, **too**. (*Too* means "also.")

The chili was **too** hot for Harry. (*Too* means "very.")

1

Write the correct word—*too, two,* or *to*—in each blank.

1. This year, Matilda wanted ___to___ attend the Chili Contest again.
2. Harry didn't want ___to___ go.
3. He said he had already been there ___two___ times.
4. Three times would be ___too___ much.
5. He wanted ___to___ see the Frog Jumping Contest instead.
6. Matilda asked if she could go, ___too___ .
7. Harry said that it would be fun if ___two___ of them attended.
8. So they both went ___to___ the Frog Jumping Contest.
9. Then Harry said he was ___too___ hungry to stay any longer.
10. So they both went ___to___ the Chili Contest and ate chili.

2 Add the correct word—*to, too,* or *two*—in each blank.

Right-Word Chili

Put a half pound of hamburger and __two__ sausages in a pot. Cook the meat over high heat until it browns. Peel and slice __two__ onions, __two__ peppers, and __two__ cloves of garlic. Put them in the pot, __too__ . Cook them until soft. Add __two__ cans of tomatoes, a can of red kidney beans, and a dash of chili powder. You don't want __to__ make it __too__ hot! Simmer 15 minutes and serve it __to__ your friends.

On Track **The recipe above is for basic chili. If you want to win the Chili Contest, you will have to add some very special ingredients. Write two sentences telling what you would add. Use *to, too,* or *two* in your sentences.**

1. Answers will vary.

____

____

____

2. ____

____

____

____

Name ______________________________

Using the Right Word 3

Homophones are words that sound alike but have different spellings and meanings. Let's look at two sets of common homophones: *its, it's* and *your, you're.*

It's vacation time.
Our school needs **its** summer "checkup."
(*It's* stands for *it is; its* shows ownership.)

You're happiest in the springtime.
(*You're* is a contraction of *you are.*)

Spring is the time when **your** puppy was born.
(*Your* shows ownership.)

Handbook Link

1 Write the correct word—*it's* or *its*—in each blank.

1. Our gym needs ___its___ clock fixed.

2. ___It's___ always slow.

3. We never know when ___it's___ time to go back to our classroom.

4. Our gym needs ___its___ water fountain checked, too.

2 Write the correct word—*you're* or *your*—in each blank.

1. Is that ___your___ puppy?

2. ___You're___ lucky to have such a nice dog.

3. You have lots of animals in ___your___ house.

4. I hope ___you're___ good at taking care of them.

On Track

Write two interesting sentences about your school. Use the homophones *it's* and *its* at least once in your sentences.

1. Answers will vary.

___

2. ___

___

Write two interesting sentences about a pet or an animal. Use the homophones *you're* and *your* at least once in your sentences.

1. Answers will vary.

___

2. ___

___

Draw a picture related to one of your sentences.

Name ______________________________

Handbook Link
316 - 321

Using the Right Word Review

1 **If the underlined homophone in each sentence is used incorrectly, cross it out and write the correct word above it. The first one has been done for you.**

aunt
1. My ~~ant~~ came to visit last weekend.

bear
2. Jon saw a ~~bare~~ at the park.

3. Be careful not to break that glass.

buy
4. I'm going to ~~by~~ a present for Sarah.

clothes
5. James left his gym ~~close~~ at home.

6. I practiced my spelling words four times.

hear
7. Did you ~~here~~ about the field trip?

8. My guinea pig ate a whole apple.

hour
9. It took me an ~~our~~ to pick a topic.

know
10. I don't ~~no~~ anyone in my new class.

11. Do rabbits eat meat?

won
12. We ~~one~~ our soccer game.

read
13. Jerry ~~red~~ his story aloud.

14. I like to write poems.

sew
15. My neighbor knows how to ~~sow~~ her own clothes.

2 **Write an interesting sentence for each homophone listed on this page.**

1. ate ______ Answers will vary. ______

   ______

   eight ______

   ______

2. hour ______

   ______

   our ______

   ______

3. knight ______

   ______

   night ______

   ______

4. your ______

   ______

   you're ______

On Track **Exchange your sentences with a classmate. Make sure that your partner has used the homophones correctly.**

2

Sentence Activities

This section includes activities related to basic sentence writing, kinds of sentences, sentence problems, and sentence combining. The On Track activities often require original writing.

Name ______________________________

Handbook Link

Simple Subjects and Predicates

The **subject** of a sentence names someone or something. The **simple subject** is the main word in the subject.

The **predicate** (verb) tells what the subject is or does. The **simple predicate** is the main word in the predicate.

simple subject → bike; simple predicate → gleams

The new <u>bike</u> <u>gleams</u> in the sun.

1

Fill in each blank with a word that makes sense. Each word you add will be the simple subject of the sentence.

1. ___Answers will vary.___ takes piano lessons.
2. ______________________ walks to school.
3. ______________________ wag their tails when they are happy.
4. My friend ______________________ has two brothers.

2

Fill in each blank with a word that makes sense. Each word you add will be the simple predicate of the sentence.

1. Ryan ___Answers will vary.___ spaghetti.
2. The teacher ______________________ us a story.
3. The sun ______________________ bright today.
4. Susie ______________________ soccer.

3 **In each sentence below, underline the simple subject once and underline the simple predicate twice. The first sentence has been done for you.**

1. Diana plays first base.
2. The thunder scared Timmy.
3. Schuyler lives next door.
4. Pizza is my favorite food.
5. Maria won.
6. Peter did the dishes.
7. Summer is the best time of year.
8. Our bus comes at 8:00 a.m.

On Track **Think of three people you know. Write one sentence about each person. Each sentence should tell something the person is or does. Underline the simple subject of each sentence once and the simple predicate twice.**

1. Answers will vary.

2.

3.

Name ______________________________

Handbook Link

Subject of a Sentence

- Every sentence has a subject. The **subject** of a sentence names something or someone.

  My old friend jumped over the candlestick.

  (*My old friend* is the complete subject.)

- The **simple subject** is the main word in the subject.

  My old friend jumped over the candlestick.

  (*Friend* is the simple subject.)

- A **compound subject** is made up of two or more simple subjects.

  Jack and Jill jumped over the candlestick.

  (*Jack* and *Jill* make up the compound subject.)

1 **Draw a line under each complete subject. Circle each simple subject. The first one has been done for you.**

1. A few little seeds fell to the ground.
2. An enormous beanstalk grew up and up.
3. Brave Jack climbed the beanstalk.
4. A huge castle rose up out of the clouds.
5. The ugly giant roared, "Fee, fie, fo, fum!"
6. The giant's wife saved Jack.
7. An old clock protected Jack from the giant.
8. Frightened little Jack stayed very still.

2 Draw a line under the complete subject in each sentence below. Write an *S* in the blank if the main part of the subject is simple or a *C* if the main part is compound. The first one has been done for you.

C 1. The giant and his wife ate dinner.

S 2. The ugly giant called for his magic goose.

S 3. The magic goose laid golden eggs.

C 4. The giant and the goose slept.

S 5. Jack snatched the goose.

S 6. The bold boy climbed down the beanstalk.

S 7. The surprised giant chased him.

S 8. Jack's mother chopped down the beanstalk.

C 9. Jack and his mother lived happily ever after.

On Track Write three sentences about a favorite fairy tale. Underline the complete subject in each sentence you write.

1. Answers will vary.

2.

3.

Name ______________________

Handbook Link

Predicate of a Sentence

- The **predicate** (verb) of a sentence tells what the subject is or does.

  Maya writes stories on her computer.

  (*Writes stories on her computer* is the complete predicate.)

- The **simple predicate** is the main word in the predicate.

  Maya writes stories on her computer.

  (*Writes* is the simple predicate.)

- A **compound predicate** is made up of two or more simple predicates.

  Maya writes stories and plays music on her computer.

  (*Writes* and *plays* make up the compound predicate.)

1

Draw two lines under each complete predicate. Circle each simple predicate, or verb. The first one has been done for you.

1. Maya thinks of good stories.
2. Maya writes about a magic keyboard.
3. The keyboard creates 100-page stories overnight.
4. Everybody loves the stories.
5. She wins dozens of prizes.
6. She becomes a great author.
7. Maya wants a magic keyboard like this.

2 **Draw two lines under the complete predicate in each sentence below. Write an *S* in the blank if the main part of the predicate is simple. Write a *C* if the main part of the predicate is compound.**

C 1. Maya sings and composes music.

S 2. Maya composes music on her computer.

C 3. She plays the melody and sings the words.

S 4. Maya's friends join her.

C 5. They sing old songs and make up new ones.

S 6. Maya's dog sings, too.

C 7. The dog barks and howls.

S 8. Maya's mother listens to the singing.

C 9. She smiles and shakes her head.

S 10. She joins in the fun.

S 11. Everyone has a good time.

On Track **Complete each thought below. Draw two lines under the complete predicates in your sentences.**

The best computer game Answers will vary. ______________________________

____.

My friends and I ______________________________

____.

Name ______________________________

Handbook Link
323-324

Subject and Predicate Review

1 **In these sentences, underline each simple subject once and underline the simple predicate twice. The first one has been done for you.**

1. Betty Bodette drives a red convertible.
2. My father drives a truck.
3. The truck belongs to a landscaping company.
4. I ride with my father sometimes.
5. My big sister comes, too.
6. We help my father.
7. He treats us to lunch at noon.

2 **Put a check in the subject box if the sentence has a compound subject. Put a check in the predicate box if the sentence has a compound predicate.**

Sentence	COMPOUND Subject	COMPOUND Predicate
1. Betty and her sister drive to the mall.	✔	
2. Betty buys a sundae and goes to the movies.		✔
3. Betty and her sister like funny movies.	✔	
4. Her brother skateboards and plays video games.		✔
5. He and his friends like to ride in the convertible.	✔	

3

Change each sentence so it has a compound subject. You will also have to change the predicate so that it agrees, or makes sense, with the new subject. The first one has been done for you.

1. Jeff walks to school.

Jeff and Jared walk to school.

2. Caroline rides on the bus.

Answers will vary.

3. Mrs. Hodorowski likes to take the train.

4. I walk with my friend Luz.

4

Change each sentence so it has a compound predicate.

1. The Lone Ranger rides a horse.

The Lone Ranger rides a horse and shoots silver bullets.

2. Mary Poppins flies with her umbrella.

Answers will vary.

3. Superman soars over the city.

Name ______________________________

Handbook Link

Simple and Compound Sentences 1

- A **simple sentence** has one main thought.

  You have two eyes.

- A **compound sentence** is two simple sentences joined by a comma and a connecting word (such as *and, but,* or *so*).

  You have two eyes, <u>and</u> they both see the same thing.

1

Carefully read the following sentences. Write an *S* in the blank for each simple sentence and a *C* for each compound sentence. The first two have been done for you.

S **1.** Miss Filbert loves science.

C **2.** She talked about eyesight, and then she did an experiment.

C **3.** Miss Filbert threw a ball to Peter, and he threw it back to her.

S **4.** She caught the ball.

S **5.** Then she put on an eye patch.

S **6.** Peter threw the ball again.

C **7.** Miss Filbert reached out to catch the ball, but she missed it.

S **8.** Miss Filbert made an important point.

C **9.** Two eyes help us see in 3-D, and they help us catch a ball.

2 Combine each set of simple sentences to make a compound sentence. The first one has been done for you.

1. Some eyes are blue. Some eyes are brown.

Some eyes are blue, and some eyes are brown.

2. A horse has two eyes. They are on the sides of its head.

A horse has two eyes, and they are on the sides of its head.

3. A human has simple eyes. A dragonfly has compound eyes.

A human has simple eyes, but a dragonfly has compound eyes.

4. Fish see underwater. Many of them see in color.

Fish see underwater, and many of them see in color.

On Track Write one simple sentence and one compound sentence about your eyes.

Simple Sentence:

Answers will vary.

Compound Sentence:

Name ______________________________

Simple and Compound Sentences 2

Handbook Link

325

- A **simple sentence** has one main thought. (Although it may have two subjects or two verbs.)

Jerry wrote a poem.
(This simple sentence has one subject and one verb.)

Jerry and Talia wrote a poem.
(This simple sentence has two subjects and one verb.)

Jerry wrote a poem and drew a picture.
(This simple sentence has one subject and two verbs.)

- A **compound sentence** is two simple sentences joined by a comma and a connecting word.

Jerry and Talia wrote a poem, and I read it.
(This compound sentence expresses two thoughts.)

1 **Carefully read each sentence. Write an *S* in the blank for each simple sentence and a *C* for each compound sentence. (*Hint:* A compound sentence must have a comma and a connecting word such as *and, or, but,* or *so.*)**

__S__ **1.** Marisa and Tom read the same book.

__S__ **2.** Charlie drew a picture and gave it to me.

__C__ **3.** I cleaned the hamster cage, and Anthony watered the plants.

__S__ **4.** The teacher and parents had a meeting.

__C__ **5.** Brittany forgot her sweater, so I loaned her mine.

__C__ **6.** It started to rain, and we closed the windows.

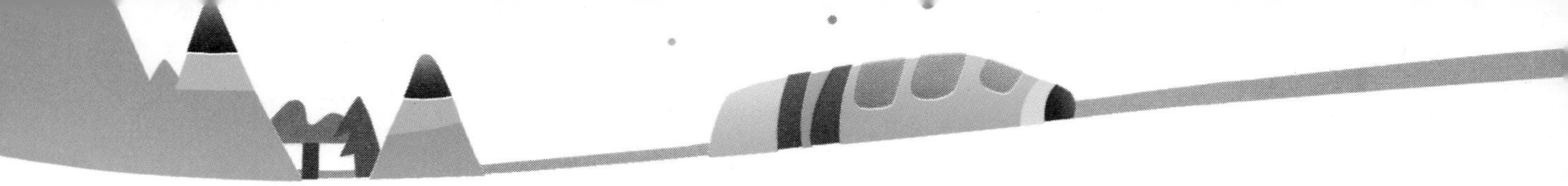

2 **Write the following types of sentences about things that have happened in your classroom.**

1. Write a simple sentence with one subject and one predicate (verb).

Answers will vary.

____

____

2. Write a simple sentence with two subjects and one verb. (Your sentence will be about two people who did one thing.)

____

____

3. Write a compound sentence. (Your sentence will be two simple sentences joined with a comma and a connecting word.)

____

____

4. Write one more compound sentence about your class.

____

____

On Track **Trade papers with a partner. Read and check each other's sentences. Make sure you followed directions correctly.**

Name ______________________________

Handbook Link 325

Declarative and Imperative Sentences

- A **declarative sentence** makes a statement.

  Leroy is a beagle.

- An **imperative statement** gives a command or makes a request.

  Leroy, sit.

  Declarative sentences and imperative sentences both end with periods.

1

Read each sentence carefully. Write *D* before each declarative sentence and *I* before each imperative sentence.

D **1.** Leroy is 13 years old.

D **2.** Thirteen is old for a dog.

I **3.** Leroy, go get the newspaper.

I **4.** Roll over, boy.

D **5.** Leroy snores.

D **6.** Leroy takes liver-flavored vitamins.

I **7.** Take your vitamin, Leroy.

2 Draw a picture of Leroy the dog. Then write some sentences about him. Write two declarative sentences that tell about Leroy. Write two imperative sentences that tell Leroy to do things.

Declarative sentences:

1. ______________________________

____

2. ______________________________

____

Imperative sentences:

1. ______________________________

____

2. ______________________________

____

Name ______________________________

Handbook Link

325

Kinds of Sentences

- A **declarative sentence** makes a statement.
  Michaelangelo was a sculptor.
- An **imperative sentence** gives a command or makes a request.
  Ask your teacher what a sculptor does.
- An **interrogative sentence** asks a question.
  Should we carve a bar of soap?
- An **exclamatory sentence** shows strong emotion or surprise.
  That's a great idea!

1 **Carefully read the sentences below. Then tell what kind of sentence each one is. Write *D* for a declarative sentence, *IN* for an interrogative sentence, *IM* for an imperative sentence, and *E* for an exclamatory sentence. The first one has been done for you.**

_D_ **1.** Sculptors make figures in stone or clay.

_IN_ **2.** Do you know any other sculptors?

_D_ **3.** Donatello was a sculptor.

_E_ **4.** I don't believe it!

_IM_ **5.** Look it up if you don't believe me.

_D_ **6.** Michaelangelo studied Donatello's sculptures.

_IN_ **7.** What was so great about Donatello?

2 **Turn each statement into a question. Add, drop, or change the order of the words to make your new sentences. The first one has been done for you.**

Answers will vary.

1. Michaelangelo lived in Italy.

   Did Michaelangelo live in Italy?

2. Michaelangelo lived about 500 years ago.

   Did Michaelangelo live about 500 years ago?

3. Michaelangelo was a painter and a sculptor.

   Was Michaelangelo a painter and a sculptor?

4. Many artists copy Michaelangelo's works.

   Do many artists copy Michaelangelo's works?

On Track **Write four sentences about a famous person. Use the four kinds of sentences: declarative, interrogative, imperative, and exclamatory.**

Declarative: Answers will vary.

Interrogative:

Imperative:

Exclamatory:

Name ______________________________

Sentence Fragments 1

Handbook Link

A complete sentence has a subject and a predicate. If either one or both of these are missing, you have a **sentence fragment**.

- In this sentence fragment, the subject is missing.

  Fragment: Jumped off the diving board.

  Corrected Sentence: Jeb jumped off the diving board.
  (A subject has been added.)

- In this sentence fragment, the subject and verb are missing.

  Fragment: In the pool.

  Corrected Sentence: Jenna and Jane swam in the pool.
  (A subject and verb have been added.)

1 **Write a *C* in front of each complete sentence below, and write an *F* in front of each sentence fragment. The first one has been done for you.**

__F__ **1.** An excellent swimmer.

__C__ **2.** Herman is an excellent swimmer.

__F__ **3.** Breaststroke, Australian crawl, and backstroke.

__C__ **4.** He is teaching me how to swim.

__C__ **5.** I am leaving.

__F__ **6.** Because of the weather.

2 Correct each sentence fragment below.

1. In the ocean.

   Missy McGee swims in the ocean.

2. Bought scuba equipment.

   Answers will vary.

3. Below the surface.

4. Colorful fish everywhere.

5. Because of the sharks.

6. Reached the boat.

On Track **Read the fragments and your sentences to a partner. Listen to the difference between a fragment and a complete sentence.**

Name ______________________________

Sentence Fragments 2

Handbook Link

Remember, a complete sentence has a subject and a predicate. If either one or both are missing, you have a **sentence fragment**.

1 **Read the paragraphs below. (If possible, read aloud with a partner.) Then underline each sentence fragment.**

Two Orphan Cubs by Erika Kors. A true story about two bear cubs. One day their mother left them forever. Gary Alt found the cubs in the den. Very hungry and lonely. Put the little bears into a sack. Took the bears to Molly's den. Molly was a bear and had two of her own cubs.

A great story. I liked it. Because there was a happy ending.

2 **Rewrite the paragraphs, using complete sentences.**

Name ______________________________

Sentence Fragments 3

Handbook Link
73

When you are using the word *because* in a sentence, make sure you don't end up with a fragment. To make a sentence, the word *because* must be combined with two complete thoughts.

Fragment: Because it had a happy ending.
Corrected Sentence: I liked it because it had a happy ending.

1

Make each sentence fragment below into a complete sentence.

1. Answers will vary. ______________ because I missed lunch.
2. ______________ because she is sick.
3. ______________ because it is my birthday.
4. ______________ because I lost my socks.
5. My friend was late because ______________.
6. I can't go because ______________.
7. He's happy because ______________.
8. I'm sorry because ______________.

On Track

Write a complete sentence on the lines below using the word *because*.

____

____

Name ______________________________

Handbook Link

Run-On Sentences 1

A **run-on sentence** happens when two or more sentences run together.

Run-On Sentence:
Mr. Wiggle's lawn mower needs repair he can't fix it.

Corrected Sentences:
Mr. Wiggle's lawn mower needs repair. He can't fix it.
(two sentences)

Mr. Wiggle's lawn mower needs repair, but he can't fix it.
(compound sentence)

1 Change each of these run-on sentences into two sentences.

1. He pulled the cord the engine didn't start.

He pulled the cord. The engine didn't start.

2. His grass was growing fast dandelions were popping up.

His grass was growing fast. Dandelions were popping up.

3. Mr. Wiggle borrowed our mower he has not returned it yet.

Mr. Wiggle borrowed our mower. He has not returned it yet.

4. I hope he gives it back soon our grass is getting very long.

I hope he gives it back soon. Our grass is getting very long.

2

Correct each run-on sentence below by rewriting the run-on as a compound sentence. (See handbook page 325.) The first one has been done for you.

1. Mr. Witt toasted some bread it burned.

   Mr. Witt toasted some bread, but it burned.

2. The smoke set off a fire alarm the fire department came.

   The smoke set off a fire alarm, and the fire department came.

3. Mr. Witt was surprised to see the firefighters he told them what happened.

   Mr. Witt was surprised to see the firefighters, and he told them what happened.

4. Mr. Witt threw out the toaster Mrs. Witt pulled it from the trash.

   Mr. Witt threw out the toaster, but Mrs. Witt pulled it from the trash.

5. Mr. Witt bought a new toaster his wife fixed the old one.

   Mr. Witt bought a new toaster, and (or but) his wife fixed the old one.

6. Now the Witts have two toasters we're thinking of borrowing one.

   Now the Witts have two toasters, so we're thinking of borrowing one.

On Track **Pair up with a classmate and check each other's compound sentences. Make sure your partner has placed a comma before the connecting word in each of his or her sentences.**

Name ______________________

Run-On Sentences 2

A run-on sentence happens when two or more sentences run together.

Run-On Sentence:
We read about Vikings they were smart.

Corrected Sentences:
We read about Vikings. They were smart.

1 Change each run-on sentence into two sentences.

1. The Vikings came to North America before Columbus they were the first Europeans to come here.

The Vikings came to North America before Columbus.

They were the first Europeans to come here.

2. Vikings were also called Norsemen northern Europe was their home.

Vikings were also called Norsemen.

Northern Europe was their home.

3. The Vikings were good sailors they were also warriors.

The Vikings were good sailors.

They were also warriors.

4. Once Vikings sailed to England their ships sailed up a river to London.

Once Vikings sailed to England.

Their ships sailed up a river to London.

2

Correct each run-on sentence by rewriting it as a compound sentence. See handbook page 325.

1. Eric the Red led Vikings to Greenland his son Leif later led Vikings to Canada.

Answers will vary.

____

____

2. No one knows why they sailed to Canada there were no towns there to raid.

____

____

3. Some experts think they were fishing a storm blew their ships off course.

____

____

On Track

Write three run-on sentence about a topic you are studying. Your sentences can be serious or silly. Trade papers with a partner and correct each other's run-ons.

1. Answers will vary.

____

2. ______________________________

____

3. ______________________________

____

Name ______________________________

Combining Sentences with a Key Word

Handbook Link

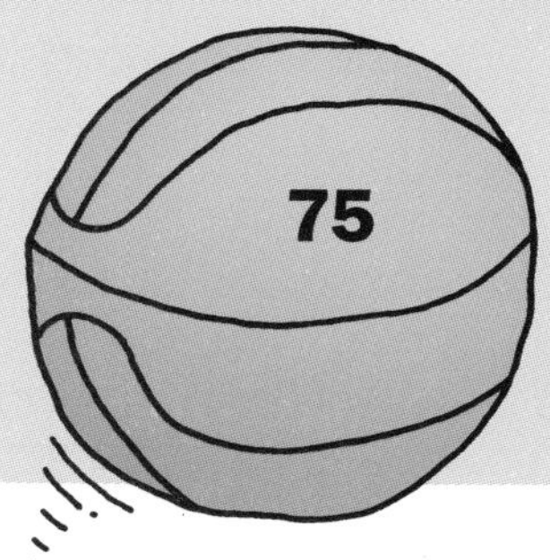

One way to combine sentences is to move a **key word** from one sentence to the other.

Short Sentences: Lizzie plays basketball.
She is on the fifth-grade team.

Combined Sentence: Lizzie plays on the fifth-grade basketball team.
(The key word is circled.)

1 **Circle the key word or words that were used to make a combined sentence. The first one has been done for you.**

1. **Short sentences:** Her team has new uniforms.
They are blue and white.

Combined sentence: Her team has new blue and white uniforms.

2. **Short sentences:** Ms. Charleyhorse is the coach.
She coaches basketball.

Combined sentence: Ms. Charleyhorse is the basketball coach.

3. **Short sentences:** The team goes to away games in a van.
The van is brand-new.

Combined sentence: The team goes to away games in a brand-new van.

4. **Short sentences:** Laura cheers for Lizzie's team.
She cheers loudly.

Combined sentence: Laura cheers loudly for Lizzie's team.

2 Combine each set of sentences below by moving a key word or words from one sentence to the other.

1. Jesse loves to roller-skate. He roller-skates every day.

   Jesse loves to roller-skate every day.

2. Jesse sometimes uses his brother's roller skates. The roller skates are green.

   Jesse sometimes uses his brother's green roller skates.

3. Jesse likes to roller-skate with his friends. He has five friends.

   Jesse likes to roller-skate with his five friends.

4. His friends are going to roller-skate with him. They will roller-skate tomorrow.

   His friends are going to roller-skate with him tomorrow.

5. Everyone will practice for a race. The race will be long.

   Everyone will practice for a long race.

On Track **Write two short sentences about one of your favorite activities. Combine your ideas into one longer sentence. (Use your own paper for your work.)**

Name ______________________

Combining Sentences with a Series of Words or Phrases 1

Handbook Link

Short Sentences: I like camping.
I like hiking.
I like swimming.

Combined Sentence: I like camping, hiking, and swimming.

1 **Fill in the blanks to complete each group of short sentences. Then combine each group to make one longer sentence.**

1. I like to play ______ Answers will vary. ______.

I like to play ______________________.

I like to play ______________________.

Combined sentence: ______________________

____

2. I like to read ______________________.

I like to read ______________________.

I like to read ______________________.

Combined sentence: ______________________

____

2 **In the space below, draw a picture of a make-believe animal. Then use words in a series to write sentences about your animal.**

1. Write a sentence telling three things your animal likes to eat.

Answers will vary.

____

____

2. Write a sentence telling three places your animal likes to hide.

____

____

3. Write a sentence telling three things your animal can do.

____

____

Name ________________________________

Combining Sentences with a Series of Words or Phrases 2

Handbook Link

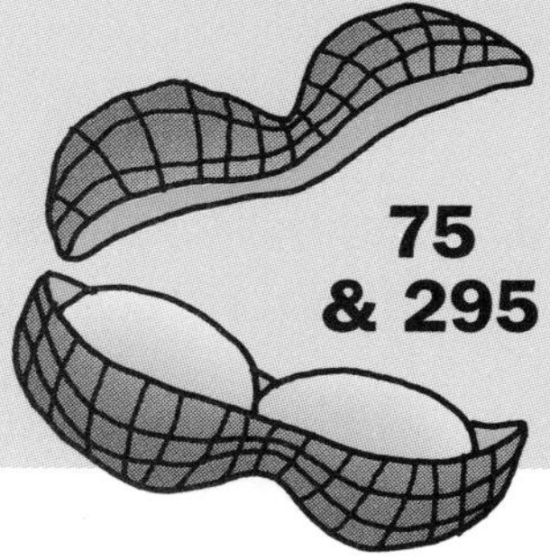

75 & 295

You can combine short sentences that tell different things about the same subject.

Short Sentences: George Washington Carver was curious. He was smart. He was hardworking.

Combined Sentence: George Washington Carver was curious, smart, and hardworking.
(The three words in a series tell different things about the subject.)

1 Combine these sentences using a series of words or phrases.

1. As a boy, George Washington Carver worked as a cook. He worked as a launderer. He worked as a janitor.

As a boy, George Washington Carver worked as a cook, a launderer, and a janitor.

2. In the laboratory, Carver found new ways to use peanuts. He found new ways to use pecans. He found new ways to use sweet potatoes.

In the laboratory, Carver found new ways to use peanuts, pecans, and sweet potatoes.

3. Carver made ink from sweet potatoes. He made flour from sweet potatoes. He made rubber from sweet potatoes.

Carver made ink, flour, and rubber from sweet potatoes.

2 Combine these sentences by using a key word from one sentence or by using words or phrases in a series.

1. Thomas Edison invented a lightbulb. He invented a phonograph. He invented a movie camera.

   Thomas Edison invented a lightbulb, a phonograph, and a movie camera.

2. Edison asked questions that began with "why." He asked questions that began with "how."

   Edison asked questions that began with "why" and "how."

3. Edison's inventions were easy to use. They were easy to keep in order. They were easy to fix.

   Edison's inventions were easy to use, to keep in order, and to fix. (or . . . to use, keep in order, and fix.)

4. He worked long hours and took only naps. The naps were short.

   He worked long hours and took only short naps.

On Track **Thomas Edison made improvements in many modern inventions, including batteries, typewriters, microphones, telephones, and radios. Write a sentence naming three of the things he helped to improve.**

Answers will vary.

Name ______________________

Combining Sentences with Compound Subjects and Verbs 1

Handbook Link

Short Sentences: LaJoy went to the circus.
Kelly went to the circus.

Combined Sentence: LaJoy and Kelly went to the circus.
(*LaJoy* and *Kelly* make up a compound subject.)

* * * * * * * * *

Short Sentences: LaJoy went to the circus.
She watched the clowns.

Combined Sentence: LaJoy went to the circus and watched the clowns.
(*Went* and *watched* make up a compound verb.)

1

Draw lines under the compound subject or the compound verb in each combined sentence.

1. **Short sentences:** Tim likes the trapeze artists.
Henry likes the trapeze artists.
Combined sentence: Tim and Henry like the trapeze artists.

2. **Short sentences:** High-wire performers ride bikes.
They walk on their hands.
Combined sentence: High-wire performers ride bikes and walk on their hands.

3. **Short sentences:** Aerialists hang by their teeth.
They twirl around.
Combined sentence: Aerialists hang by their teeth and twirl around.

2 **Combine each pair of sentences using a compound subject or a compound verb.**

1. Kelly munched popcorn. She gobbled peanuts.

   Kelly munched popcorn and gobbled peanuts.

2. Hector wanted cotton candy. His brother wanted cotton candy, too.

   Hector and his brother wanted cotton candy.

3. LaJoy bought balloons. Tim also bought balloons.

   LaJoy and Tim bought balloons.

4. Kelly bought a clown wig. She stuck it on her head.

   Kelly bought a clown wig and stuck it on her head.

On Track **Write two sentences about a circus. In one sentence, use a compound subject. In the other sentence, use a compound verb.**

Compound Subject: Answers will vary.

Compound Verb:

Name ______________________________

Combining Sentences with Compound Subjects and Verbs 2

Here's more practice using compound subjects and verbs to combine sentences.

1

Combine each group of sentences using a compound subject or verb. The first one has been done for you.

1. Once a hen lived on a farm. A cat also lived on the farm. A pig also lived on the farm.

Once a hen, a cat, and a pig lived on a farm.

2. The hen wanted to gather some wheat. She wanted to grind it into flour. She wanted to bake bread.

The hen wanted to gather some wheat, grind it into flour, and bake bread.

3. The cat refused to help her. The pig refused to help her, too.

The cat and the pig refused to help her.

4. The hen gathered the wheat all by herself. She ground it into flour all by herself. She baked bread all by herself.

The hen gathered the wheat, ground it into flour, and baked bread all by herself.

5. The cat begged for some bread. The pig begged for some, too.

The cat and the pig begged for some bread.

2 Write two sentences about the animals in the story on page 101. Use compound subjects in both of your sentences. Then write two more sentences about the animals, using compound verbs.

Sentences with compound subjects:

1. Answers will vary. ______________________

____

2. ______________________

____

Sentences with compound verbs:

1. ______________________

____

2. ______________________

____

On Track Draw a picture about one of your sentences.

Name ______________________________

Handbook Link
74-75

Sentence Combining Review 1

1 **Combine each group of sentences into one longer sentence. You can do this by moving the underlined words into the first sentence. (Sometimes you need to add the word *and*.)**

1. You may have noticed that bears have tails. Their tails are short.

   You may have noticed that bears have short tails.

2. According to legend, bears once had tails that were long. They had tails that were bushy. They had tails that were beautiful.

   According to legend, bears once had tails that were long, bushy, and beautiful.

3. Then one day a bear saw a fox. The fox was clever.

   Then one day a bear saw a clever fox.

4. The fox was eating crayfish. He was licking his lips.

   The fox was eating crayfish and licking his lips.

5. The bear asked the fox how to catch crayfish. The bear was hungry.

   The hungry bear asked the fox how to catch crayfish.

6. The fox told the bear to chop a hole in the ice. He told the bear to put his tail in the hole.

   The fox told the bear to chop a hole in the ice and put his tail in the hole.

2

Continue combining the two sentences into one longer sentence. You can do this by moving the underlined words into the first sentence. (Sometimes you need to add the word *and*.)

1. The fox told the bear to sit and wait. He told the bear to wait until a crayfish grabbed his tail.

   The fox told the bear to sit and wait until a crayfish grabbed his tail.

2. The bear went down to the frozen river. The fox went, too.

   The bear and the fox went down to the frozen river.

3. The bear followed the fox's instructions. The bear was trusting.

   The trusting bear followed the fox's instructions.

4. The ice froze around the bear's tail. It froze quickly.

   The ice quickly froze around the bear's tail.

5. The bear had to leave his tail in the ice. The ice was thick.

   The bear had to leave his tail in the thick ice.

6. That is why bears have tails that are short. Their tails are stubby. Their tails are not beautiful.

   That is why bears have tails that are short, stubby, and not beautiful.

On Track

On your own paper, write three short sentences telling what you think of the fox in this story. Then see if you can combine two or more of your sentences to make a longer sentence.

Name ______________________________

Handbook Link
74-75

Sentence Combining Review 2

In this activity you will practice all the ways you have learned to combine sentences.

1 **In the story below you will find eight underlined words or groups of words. Each of these words or groups can be moved into another sentence. Read the story aloud and combine sentences as you go along.**

Last February, my dad and I were pulling down a chicken coop in our backyard. The chicken coop was old. I ripped off a board. I saw something.

"What's that?" I said.

"It's just a pile of old rags. They're gray," my dad said.

Then I yanked off another board and saw something. It was pink. It was squishy looking.

"Dad, can gray rags have a pink nose?"

Finally, Dad looked into the chicken coop. He looked carefully. "It's a possum! We just woke up a possum. It was sleeping."

The possum walked away like it was dizzy. Then it disappeared into the woods. Dad laughed. I laughed, too.

2 **Now rewrite the story from page 105. Combine some of the sentences, using the underlined words and phrases.**

____

____

____

____

____

____

____

____

____

____

____

____

____

____

____

On Track

Turn to page 83 in your handbook. Compare your story to the way Adam Kendall wrote it. Your story may be a little different. That's okay, because there's more than one way to combine sentences!

3

Language Activities

The activities in this section are related to the eight parts of speech. All of the activities have a page link to *Write on Track*.

Name ______________________________

Nouns

A **noun** names a person, a place, a thing, or an idea. The following lists are nouns that belong to each of the four groups.

Person	Place	Thing	Idea
bride	street	bicycle	joy
boy	pool	flowerpot	truth
friend	school	horse	hope
coach	park	whale	sadness

Handbook Link

1 **Complete each sentence below by adding nouns from the lists above. (Your sentences can be as silly as you want to make them.) The first one has been done for you.**

1. The ___bride___ hopped over the ___flowerpot___ .

2. My ___Answers will vary.___ tells the ______________ .

3. The ______________ is in the ______________ .

4. A ______________ has lots of ______________ .

5. The ______________ sang to the ______________ .

6. Look at the ______________ riding a ______________ .

7. John told his ______________ to go to the ______________ .

8. Myra saw a ______________ on the ______________ .

9. The ______________ is full of ______________ .

2

Draw a line under the two nouns in each of these sentences. The first sentence has been done for you.

1. The clown sings in the bathtub.
2. The gorilla rides a skateboard.
3. The chef cooked a buzzard.
4. That kid lives in Overshoe.
5. The cowboy roped a skunk.
6. Sarah sang with joy.
7. This path leads to the cave.
8. Mary dreamed of flying cows.
9. The runner has lots of hope.

On Track

Draw a picture for one of the sentences you worked with in this activity.

Name ______________________________

Common and Proper Nouns

Handbook Link

- A **common noun** names any person, place, thing, or idea.

  man country book

- A **proper noun** names a specific person, place, thing, or idea.

  Mr. Taylor Mexico Write on Track

1 **Match each group of proper nouns to a common noun. The first one has been done for you.**

	Common Nouns		Proper Nouns
h	**1.** states	**a.**	Canada, Mexico, United States
f	**2.** songs	**b.**	Venus, Mars, Earth
a	**3.** countries	**c.**	Lake Michigan, Great Salt Lake, Lake Okeechobee
e	**4.** mountains	**d.**	Steve, John, Jim
c	**5.** lakes	**e.**	Rocky Mountains, Blue Ridge Mountains, Ozark Mountains
d	**6.** boys	**f.**	"The Star-Spangled Banner," "America the Beautiful," "This Land Is Your Land"
b	**7.** planets	**g.**	Missouri River, Snake River, Yukon River
i	**8.** languages	**h.**	Hawaii, Alaska, California
g	**9.** rivers	**i.**	English, Spanish, Mandarin Chinese
j	**10.** books	**j.**	*Write on Track, Strega Nona, Where the Wild Things Are*

2

After each common noun, write a proper noun that goes with it. Your proper nouns can name real people, places, and things, or they can be made-up names.

Common Nouns	Proper Nouns
1. doctor	Answers will vary.
2. cat	
3. park	
4. book	
5. store	
6. girl	
7. team	
8. city	
9. river	
10. movie	
11. boy	
12. teacher	

On Track

On your own paper, write a paragraph using some of the nouns above. After you finish, label each common noun *C* and each proper noun *P*.

Name ______________________

Singular and Plural Nouns

- A **singular noun** names one person, place, thing, or idea.

  farmer   park   car   freedom

Write two more singular nouns here.

Answers will vary.

- A **plural noun** names more than one person, place, thing, or idea.

  farmers   parks   cars   freedoms

Write two more plural nouns here.

Answers will vary.

1 **Draw one line under each noun in the sentences below. Label each singular noun *S* and each plural noun *P*. The first one has been done for you.**

1. My children (P) work in the theater (S).
2. Elizabeth (S) acts in plays (P).
3. Her brother (S) paints the sets (P).
4. The theater (S) is on Hill Street (S).
5. Two new shows (P) just opened.
6. Sean (S) had free tickets (P).
7. The audience (S) laughed at the jokes (P).

2 **Write five singular nouns in the first column. Then write the plural of each noun in the second column.**

singular	plural
1. ______	______
2. ______	______
3. ______	______
4. ______	______
5. ______	______

Answers will vary.

Write two interesting sentences using singular nouns from your list.

1. Answers will vary.
______
______

2. ______
______

Write two interesting sentences using plural nouns from your list.

1. Answers will vary.
______
______

2. ______
______

Name ______________________________

Personal Pronouns 1

A **pronoun** is a word that takes the place of a noun.

Sam wrote a letter and mailed it.
(The pronoun *it* replaces the noun *letter*.)

Sam opened the mailbox, and he found a letter from Andy.
(The pronoun *he* replaces the noun *Sam*.)

Handbook Link

Common Personal Pronouns

Singular Pronouns	Plural Pronouns
I, me, my	we, our, us
you, your	you, your
he, him, his, hers	they, their, them
she, her, it, its	

1 **List below the personal pronouns in the sample paragraph on page 63 in the handbook. The first two have been done for you.**

1. Our
2. It
3. them
4. We
5. our
6. our
7. us
8. We
9. our
10. we
11. our
12. We
13. our
14. we

2 **In each sentence below, change the crossed-out name or names to a personal pronoun. The first one has been done for you.**

they

1. Tracy and Gaby started a newspaper, and ~~Tracy and Gaby~~ write all the stories.

her

2. Gaby uses ~~Gaby's~~ mom's computer.

she them

3. Tracy and Gaby interviewed the teacher, and ~~the teacher~~ told ~~Tracey and Gaby~~ about her new piano.

her

4. The teacher told Tracy and Gaby about ~~the teacher's~~ music lessons.

their

5. The girls think it is neat that ~~the girls'~~ teacher is learning something new.

We

6. Gaby said, "~~Tracy and Gaby~~ like our teacher a lot."

On Track **Write three sentences about something you and your friends do after school. In each sentence, use at least one personal pronoun.**

1. Answers will vary.
____
____

2. ____
____

3. ____
____

Name ____________________

Handbook Link

Personal Pronouns 2

A **pronoun** is a word that replaces a noun.

1

In each of the sentences, write the name of the person that the underlined pronoun stands for. Write Lori or Pam.

One day Lori was playing kickball in the backyard.

1. After a few minutes, she heard Pam calling her.

Lori ____________ Lori ____________

2. Pam was calling from her yard, but Lori couldn't see her.

Pam ____________ Pam ____________

3. Lori called, "Do you want to play kickball with me?"

Pam ____________ Lori ____________

4. "I sure do," answered Pam. And she ran right over.

Pam ____________ Pam ____________

2

Fill in personal pronouns for the next part of the story.

Answers may vary.

Lori and Pam had lots of fun. When ___they___ finished playing kickball, the girls went into the house. Lori's mom gave ___them___ a treat. Pam said, "Thank ___you___. ___We___ sure had fun at ___your___ house today."

3 **Circle all of the pronouns you find in this paragraph. (There are 19 pronouns all together.)**

Living with a Little Brother

Living with my little brother can be hard. First, he tries to copy me. If I have a second glass of milk, he does, too. Second, he always wants to play with my friends. If we play basketball, he wants to join in. But he is too small. Third, he wants to stay up as long as I do. He always says to my mom, "But Tim gets to stay up later." My mom says that he looks up to me, and I should be proud to be his big brother.

On Track **Write a short paragraph about someone in your family. Circle all of the pronouns you use.**

Answers will vary.

Name ______________________________

Pronouns: I and Me, They and Them

Handbook Link

A **pronoun** is a word that replaces a noun. *I* and *me* are pronouns. *They* and *them* are also pronouns.

I **is used as the subject of a sentence.**

I lost the key.

Me **is used after an action verb or after a preposition.**

Angelo called me. Mom baked cookies for me.

They **is used as the subject of a sentence.**

They are friends.

Them **is used after an action verb or after a preposition.**

The lightning scares them. Sophie had a surprise for them.

1 Write the correct word, *I* or *me*, in each blank.

1. ___I___ need a haircut.

2. Daniel called ___me___.

3. Janelle asked ___me___ for a marker.

4. ___I___ finished my homework.

5. Carla did my chores for ___me___.

2 Write the correct word, *they* or *them,* in each blank.

1. I invited ___them___ to my party.

2. ___They___ like to read stories.

3. I visit ___them___ every Saturday.

4. We made a present for ___them___.

5. ___They___ are my cousins.

3 Choose the correct word from each pair and write it in the blank.

___I___ *(I, Me)* made two bracelets and gave ___them___ *(they, them)* to Maggie. ___They___ *(They, Them)* are made from glass beads. My sister showed ___me___ *(I, me)* how to make ___them___ *(they, them)*. Maggie's parents told ___me___ *(I, me)* the bracelets were very pretty. ___They___ *(They, Them)* said ___I___ *(I, me)* should keep making ___them___ *(they, them)*. ___They___ *(They, Them)* said ___I___ *(I, me)* could sell ___them___ *(they, them)* at the craft show.

4 Write three sentences about a game you play with a friend. Use as many pronouns as you can.

1. Answers will vary.

2. ______________________

3. ______________________

Name ______________________________

Handbook Link

Action and Linking Verbs

- An **action verb** tells what the subject does or did.

  Ripe apples drop off trees.

  I ate a piece of apple pie.

- A **linking verb** links the subject to a word in the predicate.

  Apples are fruit.

  That apple pie was delicious!

1 Write an action verb in each sentence.

1. Apple trees __Answers will vary.__ in late spring.

2. I ______________________ apples in the fall.

3. Once I ______________________ a worm in an apple.

4. My mom ______________________ apple butter.

2 Write a linking verb in each sentence.

1. Applesauce __Answers will vary.__ soft and delicious.

2. Granny Smith apples ______________________ green.

3. I ______________________ an apple fan!

4. Last year, the orchard ______________________ full of apples.

3

Draw two lines under the verb in each sentence. Write an *A* in the blank if the verb shows action or an *L* if the verb links two words. The first one has been done for you.

A 1. Johnny Appleseed learned about apples.

L 2. Johnny Appleseed's real name was John Chapman.

A 3. Johnny walked through the Midwest.

A 4. He wore a sack as a shirt.

A 5. He planted many, many apple trees.

L 6. Johnny Appleseed was well-known.

A 7. Many people wrote books about him.

L 8. Some books about Johnny Appleseed are tall tales.

On Track **Write three sentences about apples. Use at least one of the verbs below in each sentence.**

eat peel chop cut taste is be are was slice

1. Answers will vary.

2. ______

3. ______

Name ______________________

Handbook Link

329

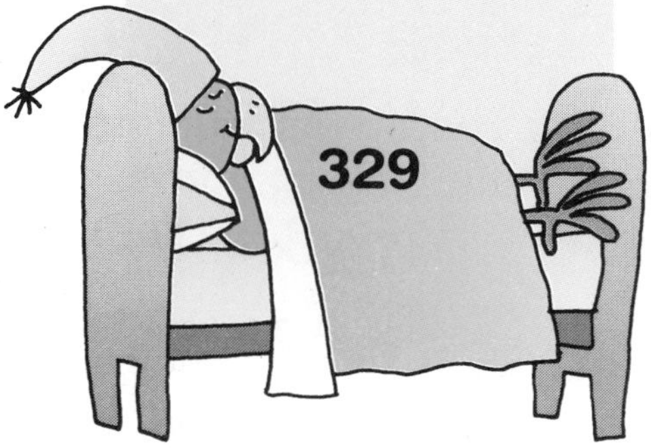

Helping Verbs

A **helping verb** comes before the main verb and helps to state an action or show time.

Helping Verbs: can, could, did, do, had, has, have, may, should, will, would

1 **Draw two lines under the helping verb and action verb in each sentence. The first one has been done for you.**

1. Parrots can sleep standing up.
2. Humpback whales do make a lot of noise.
3. Australians have named baby kangaroos "joeys."
4. A baby elephant will grow quickly.
5. Swans do eat plants, insects, and small fish.

2 **Write two sentences. Each sentence should contain one of the action verbs listed below, plus a helping verb. Draw two lines under each helping verb and action verb.**

run push eat called

Example: An elephant can eat a lot.

1. Answers will vary.

____

2. ______________________

____

Name ______________________

Handbook Link
329

Reviewing Verbs

- There are two main types of verbs, **action verbs** and **linking verbs**.

  I fed my dog. (*Fed* is an action verb.)

  He is hungry. (*Is* is a linking verb.)

- Sometimes a **helping verb** is used with an action verb or a linking verb.

  My dog will eat anything.

1 **Draw two lines under the main verb in each sentence. Write an *A* in the blank if the verb shows action or an *L* if the verb links two words. The last two sentences contain helping verbs. For those sentences, underline the helping verbs along with the main verbs.**

A **1.** My dog runs fast.

A **2.** My dog acts like a person.

L **3.** His name is Bob.

L **4.** We are so happy with Bob.

A **5.** He plays in the kitchen.

A **6.** My baby sister Nina loves Bob.

A **7.** She sits in the kitchen with him.

A **8.** Once she tasted Bob's dog food.

A **9.** Nina should eat her own food!

L **10.** Bob will be our friend forever.

Name ______________________________

Verb Tenses 1

Handbook Link

- A verb in the **present tense** tells you that the action takes place now, or that it happens all the time.

  I hear a cricket singing.

  A cricket hops across the lawn.

- A verb in the **past tense** tells you that the action happened in the past.

  Yesterday a cricket hopped onto my leg.

1 **Carefully read each sentence. Write present in the blank if the underlined verb is in the present tense, or past if it is in the past tense.**

present 1. Crickets sing by rubbing their wings together.

present 2. My grandfather keeps a singing cricket in a cage.

present 3. It tells the temperature.

present 4. On hot days it chirps fast.

past 5. I heard the cricket chirp a few minutes ago.

past 6. It chirped 50 times in 15 seconds.

past 7. I tried to chirp myself.

past 8. I sounded really stupid.

present 9. Chirping gives me a sore throat.

2

Each present-tense verb in the following sentences is underlined. On each blank, write the past tense of the verb. Then read the sentence with the new verb in it.

Present Tense	Past Tense
1. Jiminy Cricket meets Tinkerbell.	met
2. He helps Pinocchio.	helped
3. Jiminy talks about right from wrong.	talked
4. Pinocchio needs Jiminy.	needed
5. He whistles for Jiminy.	whistled
6. Jiminy Cricket hops to his side.	hopped
7. Then Jiminy calls for Geppetto.	called
8. Pinocchio likes Jiminy.	liked

On Track

Write two sentences about insects. Use a present-tense verb in one sentence and a past-tense verb in the other.

Present tense Answers will vary. ____________________

____

Past tense ____________________

____

Name ______________________________

Verb Tenses 2

- Remember that a verb in the **present tense** tells you that the action takes place now, or that it happens all the time.

  It snows.

  I make a snowman.

- A verb in the **future tense** tells you that the action will take place at a later time.

  The sun will come out.

  It will melt the snow.

Handbook Link

1

After each sentence, check whether the underlined verb is in the present tense or in the future tense. The first one has been done for you.

	PRESENT	FUTURE
1. I see snow falling.	✓	
2. Snow falls softly and silently.	✓	
3. It covers roads and roofs.	✓	
4. I hope that it snows all night.	✓	
5. Then they will close the schools.		✓
6. I will have to shovel snow.		✓
7. I will clear the walk.		✓
8. Then I will build a snow fort.		✓
9. That sounds like fun!	✓	

2 **Draw two lines under the verb in each sentence. Write present in the blank if the verb is in the present tense, future if it is in the future tense. The first one has been done for you.**

future 1. What will melt snow?

present 2. Salt melts snow.

future 3. Dan's experiment will prove it.

present 4. Dan fills two cans with snow or ice.

present 5. He dumps salt on the snow in one can.

present 6. He sets a timer for one hour.

future 7. Then he will look at the cans.

On Track **Change each of the following sentences to the future tense. Then write one more sentence about snow. Use the future tense in your new idea.**

1. Snow falls.

   Snow will fall.

2. It clings to branches and twigs.

   It will cling to branches and twigs.

3. Soon the world looks like a giant wedding cake.

   Soon the world will look like a giant wedding cake.

4. Answers will vary.

Name ______________________________

Verb Tenses 3

The **tense** of a verb tells you if the action happened in the present, past, or future.

Present Tense:

Peter picks a peck of pickled peppers.

Past Tense:

Peter picked a peck of pickled peppers yesterday.

Future Tense:

Peter will pick a peck of pickled peppers tomorrow.

1 **Draw two lines under the verb in each of the following tongue twisters. Then, in the blank space, write past, present, or future for the tense of the verb. The first sentence has been done for you.**

past **1.** A big black bug bit a big black bear.

past **2.** Three gray geese grazed in the green grass.

past **3.** Teddy took two turtles to Todd's house.

present **4.** Barbara always burns the brown bread.

past **5.** A fly flew through the flue.

future **6.** The dog will choose to chew the shoes.

future **7.** She will sip a cup of hot cinnamon cider.

present **8.** I love little lightning bugs.

present **9.** Carol collects colorful cups.

Present	Past	Future
run	ran	will run
sells	sold	will sell
close	closed	will close
bubbles	bubbled	will bubble
take	took	will take
watch	watched	will watch

2 **Create your own tongue twisters by completing the sentences below. Select verbs from the list above. The first one has been done for you.**

1. The ragged rascal ___ran___ around the rocks.
(past)

2. She ___sold___ seashells by the seashore.
(past)

3. Rosie and Rory ___run___ around the roller rink.
(present)

4. Clyde's Clothes Closet ___will close___ for cleaning.
(future)

5. Double bubble gum ___will bubble___ double.
(future)

6. Tim ___took___ a turn on Tammy's tandem.
(past)

7. Wally ___watched___ the walrus in the water.
(past)

On Track **Share your tongue twisters with a classmate. Write more examples to share. (Use your own paper.)**

Name ______________________________

Regular Verbs

- Add *-ed* to regular verbs to form the past tense.

  Willy and Milly sailed the boat last summer.

- Also add *-ed* to regular verbs when you use a helping verb such as *has, have,* or *had.*

  Willy had sailed for years.

Handbook Link

* * * * * * * * *

- If a regular verb ends in *e*, just add *d* to form the past tense.

  raise ········► raised

- If a one-syllable verb ends in a single consonant, double the consonant and add *-ed.*

  shop ········► shopped

1 Write these regular verbs in the past tense.

1. hop hopped
2. hope hoped
3. name named
4. tap tapped
5. skip skipped
6. raise raised
7. talk talked
8. hum hummed
9. push pushed
10. save saved
11. flip flipped
12. splash splashed
13. stop stopped
14. giggle giggled
15. lick licked
16. drip dripped

2 **In each set of sentences below, study the underlined verb in the first sentence. Then write the *-ed* (past tense) form of the underlined verb to complete the second sentence. The first one has been done for you.**

1. They call the boat the *Lilly*.

They called it the *Lilly* two years ago.

2. Milly and Willy row out to the *Lilly*.

Yesterday, they rowed out to the *Lilly*.

3. Milly raises the *Lilly's* sail.

Last year, she raised it every morning.

4. Milly and Willy love to sail the *Lilly*.

Milly and Willy always have loved to sail the *Lilly*.

5. Milly drops the anchor.

Willy gave the signal, and Milly dropped the anchor.

6. Willy cleans the *Lilly* once a week.

He had cleaned it two days before the storm.

On Track **Draw a picture including Milly, Willy, and the *Lilly*.**

Name ______________________________

Singular and Plural Verbs

The subject of a sentence can be singular or plural. Notice how the verb *plays* changes when the subject changes from singular to plural.

Caleb plays basketball at the park.
(singular verb)

His friends play with him.
(plural verb)

Handbook Link

1 Write the correct form of the verb in each sentence.

1. practices practice

Jake, Caleb, and Rhonda ___practice___ shooting baskets every day.

Sometimes Jake even ___practices___ at night.

2. dribbles dribble

Caleb ___dribbles___ the ball across the court.

Then Jake and Rhonda ___dribble___ it.

3. tosses toss

Rhonda ___tosses___ the ball, and she misses.

Caleb and Jake ___toss___ and miss.

4. jumps jump

The boys ___jump___ for the rebound.

Rhonda ___jumps___, too.

2 **Write your own sentences using the singular and plural verbs listed.**

1. passes pass

Answers will vary.

2. scores score

3. cheers cheer

4. joins join

5. chooses choose

On Track **Draw two lines under all of the singular verbs. What do you notice about all of them?**

Name ______________________________

Irregular Verbs

Handbook Link

1 Study the irregular verbs in the handbook. As a class, complete the sentences below with the correct forms of the irregular verb.

1. begin

present: I ___begin___ school at 8:30.

past: Last year, school ___began___ at 8:00.

past with *had*: When I got there, school had ___begun___ .

2. am

present: I ___am___ in the third grade.

past: Last year, I ___was___ in second grade.

past with *have*: I have ___been___ looking forward to third grade.

3. catch

present: I ___catch___ a lot of balls at softball practice.

past: In my last game, I ___caught___ a fly ball.

past with *had*: I had ___caught___ two fly balls in other games.

4. hide

present: I ___hide___ from my brother sometimes.

past: Last night, I ___hid___ in my closet.

past with *have*: I have ___hidden (or hid)___ there before.

2 **Now complete the following sets of sentences on your own. The directions are the same as in part 1.**

1. fly

present: I ___fly___ to Minneapolis every summer.

past: Last year, I ___flew___ by myself.

past with *have:* I have ___flown___ for years with my dad.

2. come

present: Most days, I ___come___ to school with my sister.

past: Yesterday, I ___came___ by myself.

past with *have:* I have ___come___ by myself two other times.

3. throw

present: I ___throw___ practice pitches every Friday.

past: Last Friday, I ___threw___ 30 pitches.

past with *had:* I had ___thrown___ 25 pitches before I hurt my arm.

On Track **Write two sentences of your own using different forms of the verb *speak.***

1. Answers will vary.

____

2. ______________________________

____

Name ______________________

Verbs Review

Handbook Link
329-332

An **action verb** tells what someone or something does.

Jenny <u>hits</u> lots of home runs.

The wind <u>blows</u> down our fort.

1 **List three action verbs below. Trade papers with a partner. Then write two sentences for each of your partner's action verbs—one singular and one plural.**

1. Action verb: Answers will vary.
Sentence with singular verb:

____

Sentence with plural verb:

____

2. Action verb: ______________________
Sentence with singular verb:

____

Sentence with plural verb:

____

3. Action verb: ______________________
Sentence with singular verb:

____

Sentence with plural verb:

____

2 **In the paragraph below, change each underlined verb to past tense. The first one has been done for you.**

Dennis rings (rang) the doorbell and then runs (ran) away and hides (hid). I see (saw) him and tell (told) my mom. She says (said) Dennis does (did) it because he likes (liked) me. Maybe she is (was) right. Dennis also rides (rode) his bike past our house and brings (brought) our newspaper to the door.

On Track **Write some more sentences about Dennis, using the verbs given. First write a sentence in the present tense. Then write a sentence in the past tense.**

1. Verb: write

Sentence in present tense: Answers will vary. ______________________

____

Sentence in past tense: ____

____

2. Verb: go

Sentence in present tense: ____

____

Sentence in past tense: ____

____

Name ______________________________

Handbook Link
333-334

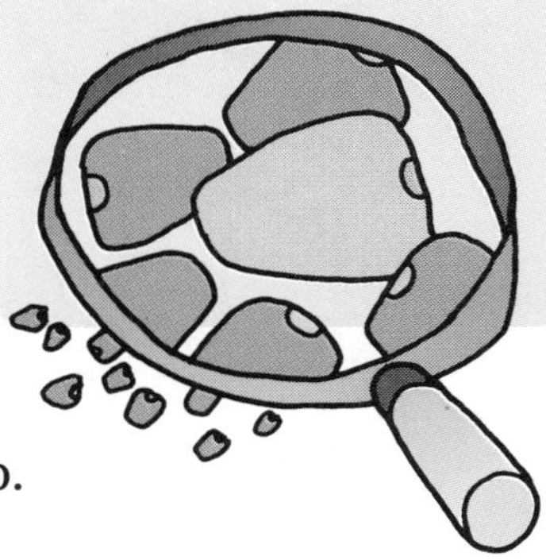

Adjectives 1

- An **adjective** usually comes before the noun it describes.

  Carrie planted tiny seeds.

  What noun does the adjective *tiny* describe in this sentence? seeds

- Sometimes an **adjective** comes after a linking verb.

  The seeds were tiny.

  What noun does the adjective *tiny* describe in this sentence? seeds

1 **Underline the adjective in each sentence. Then draw an arrow to the noun it describes. (Don't include the words *a, an,* or *the.*) The first one has been done for you.**

1. She used a sharp spade to dig.
2. Carrie planted red zinnias.
3. She watered the little seeds.
4. Green leaves soon popped up.
5. Bright sun shone on the plants.
6. Gentle rain watered them.
7. Fat buds formed.
8. Soon Carrie could pick a pretty bouquet of zinnias.

2

Draw a line under each adjective in the following sentences. Then draw an arrow to the noun it describes. All of these adjectives come after a linking verb. The first one has been done for you.

1. Roses are red.
2. Violets are blue.
3. Sugar is sweet.
4. Words are true.
5. Daisies are white.
6. Marigolds are yellow.
7. Honey is sweet.
8. Sarah sure is mellow.

On Track

Write a sentence for each adjective-noun pair.

Adjectives	Nouns
fluffy →	kitten
tough →	guy
beautiful →	song
silver →	earrings

1. Answers will vary. ______________________________

____

2. ______________________________

____

3. ______________________________

____

4. ______________________________

____

Name ______________________________

Handbook Link

Adjectives 2

An adjective is a word that describes a noun or a pronoun.

- An **adjective** usually comes before the noun it describes.

  Auntie Grimelda has blue hair.
  (*Blue* describes *hair.*)

- Sometimes an **adjective** comes after a linking verb.

  Auntie Grimelda's hair is blue.

1 **On your own paper, draw a picture of a person. Imagine that this person is going to be the main character in a fantasy story. Put lots of details in your drawing. Use lots of colors. (And give your person a name.) After you finish, list adjectives below to describe the person you drew.**

hair	face	eyes
________	________	________
________	________	________
nose	**mouth**	**ears**
________	________	________
________	________	________
body	**clothes**	**voice**
________	________	________
________	________	________

2 Trade pictures and your list of adjectives with a classmate. Look closely at your partner's drawing. Add some adjectives to your partner's list.

On Track Trade papers again so that you have your own drawing and the adjectives that describe it. Write a paragraph that describes the person you drew. Use as many of your adjectives as you can. (See handbook page 61.)

Answers will vary.

Name ______________________________

Handbook Link

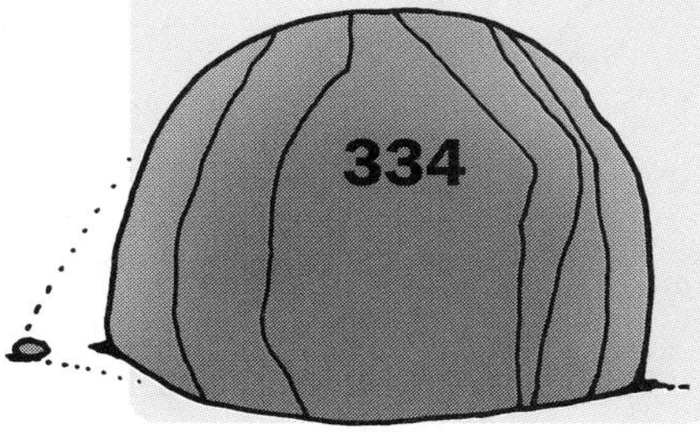

Forms of Adjectives

Adjectives have three different forms.

Positive: This pebble is <u>small</u>.

Comparative: This pebble is <u>smaller</u> than that rock.

Superlative: This pebble is the <u>smallest</u> stone in my collection.

1 Write sentences for the forms of the adjectives listed below.

loud, louder, loudest

1. Answers will vary.

2. ______________________________

____

3. ______________________________

____

happy, happier, happiest

1. Answers will vary.

2. ______________________________

____

3. ______________________________

____

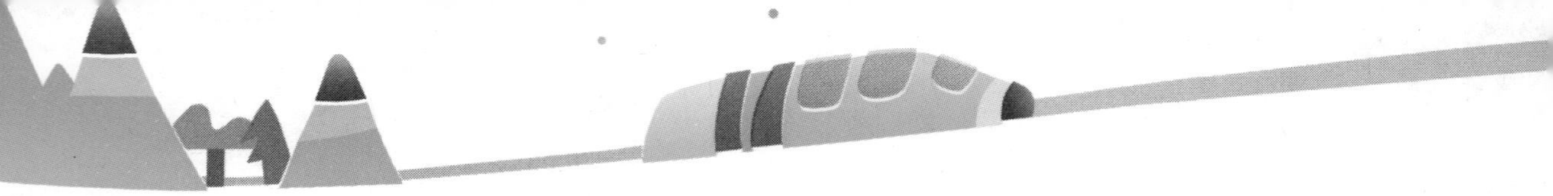

2 **Write a paragraph about a beautiful or interesting place you have visited. Use plenty of adjectives in your writing.**

Answers will vary.

On Track **Circle the adjectives in your paragraph. Did you write any adjectives in the comparative (ending in *er*) or the superlative form (ending in *est*)?**

Name ______________________________

Adverbs 1

An **adverb** is a word that describes a verb, or tells how an action is done. Adverbs usually tell *when, where,* or *how*.

- Some adverbs that tell *when:*
  always, never, soon, weekly
- Some adverbs that tell *where:*
  outside, there, up
- Some adverbs that tell *how:*
  slowly, loudly, jokingly

Handbook Link

1

Circle the adverb in each sentence. Then write whether it tells *when, where,* or *how.* The first one has been done for you.

1. Jeremy (always) eats his cabbage. when
2. Karen goes to bed (early.) when
3. Rags comes (quickly) when he is called. how
4. Shari (never) teases her little brother. when
5. Todd goes to the dentist (cheerfully.) how
6. Michelle cleans her room (daily.) when
7. I took the trash (outside.) where
8. Sean makes his bed (carefully.) how
9. Emily comes (here) for lunch. where

2

Cross out the adverb in each sentence. Replace it with a different adverb that changes the meaning of the sentence. The first one has been done for you.

jokingly
1. "I'll ride a bike," Mom said ~~seriously~~.

loudly
2. Sparky snores ~~softly~~.

often
3. Cal ~~seldom~~ sees his cousins.

sadly, angrily
4. Tamika did her chores ~~happily~~.

often, always
5. Maria is ~~never~~ late for school.

noisily, loudly
6. "Those boys are playing so ~~quietly~~," said Granddad.

away, outside
7. Fuzzy stays ~~nearby~~ when he knows it's bath time.

On Track **Write three sentences about yourself.**

1. Use the adverb *someday* (when).

Answers will vary.

____

____

2. Use the adverb *outside* (where).

____

____

3. Use the adverb *slowly* (how).

____

____

Name ______________________________

Adverbs 2

Handbook Link

An **adverb** is a word that describes a verb, or tells how an action is done. Adverbs usually answer *when* (adverb of time), *where* (adverb of place), or *how* (adverb of manner).

1

Adverbs of time tell *when* or *how often* an action is done. Fill in the blank in each sentence with one adverb from the list below.

yesterday	soon	now	first
tomorrow	later	weekly	last

1. Our class went to the toy museum Answers will vary.
2. I hope we can go back again ______________________.
3. In fact, I wish we could go ______________________.

2

Adverbs of place tell *where* something happens. Fill in the blank in each sentence with one adverb from the list below.

inside	here	up
outside	there	down

1. I told my mom I wanted to go Answers will vary. to play.
2. She looked ______________________ at me.
3. "Why don't you just play ______________________?" she asked.

3 **Adverbs of manner tell *how* something is done. Fill in the blank in each sentence with one adverb from the list below.**

quietly	carefully	slowly	happily
loudly	carelessly	quickly	sadly

1. I like to play my cassette player Answers will vary.

2. When I clean up my room, I do it very ____________.

3. When it's time to eat, my cat comes running ____________.

On Track **Write four adverbs. Then write a paragraph that has all four adverbs in it.**

1. Answers will vary.

2. ____________

3. ____________

4. ____________

Name

Prepositions

A phrase that begins with a preposition and ends with a noun is called a **prepositional phrase**.

to the lighthouse
in the boat
under the bridge
across the water
after breakfast

Handbook Link

1

Draw a line under the prepositional phrase in each sentence below. Then circle each preposition. The first one has been done for you.

1. Ray was in deep water.
2. Ray was swimming against the tide.
3. He went backward with every stroke.
4. Waves washed over his head.
5. He was not near the beach.
6. Just then, he felt the nudge of a boat.
7. A lifeguard threw him a life preserver on a rope.
8. Ray reached for the rope.
9. The lifeguard rowed Ray toward the beach.
10. Ray said, "Thank you. I was really in danger."

2

Draw a line under the prepositional phrases in the sentences below. Then circle each preposition. (Some of these sentences have more than one prepositional phrase.) The first one has been done for you.

1. Pay attention to these rules about water safety.
2. Swim at beaches protected by lifeguards.
3. Never jump into strange waters.
4. Always look for underwater obstacles.
5. Do not swim in unmarked areas or in bad weather.
6. Always swim close to the shore and with a friend.
7. Go slowly into cold water.
8. Swim with other people.
9. Stay inside the buoys.

On Track **Create a sign for one of the safety rules above.**

Name ______________________________

Handbook Link

Conjunctions

A **conjunction** connects words or groups of words. The most common conjunctions are *and, but,* and *or.* There are three conjunctions in the following sentence:

Charley (and) Barbara wore their coats (and) hats, (but) they forgot their boots.

1 Draw a circle around the 10 conjunctions in this story.

The Sun (and) the Wind

Who is stronger, the sun (or) the wind? Well, once upon a time, each one thought it was stronger, (so) they had a contest.

"I am strong enough to make that man take off his hat, his scarf, (and) his coat," bragged the wind. The sun said nothing. It just hid behind a cloud.

The wind blew (and) blew, (but) the man did not take off his hat, his scarf, (or) his coat. Instead, he pulled them tighter (and) tighter to his body.

Then the sun came out brightly (but) quietly. Soon the man grew warm. He took off his hat, (and) he took off his scarf. Then he removed his coat.

Now do you know who is stronger? Is it the sun (or) the wind?

On Track **Write a sentence that answers the last two questions in the story.**

Answers will vary.

____

Name ______________________________

Interjections

Hey! Let me tell you about interjections. An **interjection** is a word or phrase used to express strong emotion or surprise. It is usually followed by an exclamation point.

Handbook Link

1 **Draw a picture or design for each interjection and sentence. Write your own sentence with an interjection in the last box. Draw a picture for it, too.**

Answers will vary.

Hey! I did it!	Wow, I can't believe I just saw that!
Yuck! Look at all the bugs!	

Name ______________________

Handbook Link
326-337

Parts of Speech Review

This activity is a review of the parts of speech.

1 **Write three examples of each part of speech. Do as many as you can on your own. Then ask a classmate for help or check your handbook.**

Nouns
(Name a person, place, thing, or idea)

____
____
____

Pronouns
(Take the place of nouns)

Answers will vary.
____
____

Verbs
(Show action or link ideas)

____
____
____

Adjectives
(Describe a noun or pronoun)

____
____
____

Adverbs
(Describe a verb; tell how an action is done)

____
____
____

Conjunctions
(Connect words or groups of words)

____
____
____

Prepositions
(Introduce a prepositional phrase)

____
____
____

Interjections
(Express strong emotion or surprise)

____
____
____

On Track

In the space below, draw a picture that shows this sentence:

The shiny red spaceship rocketed to the stars!

Copy the sentence under your drawing. Then label each word to show what part of speech it is.